GOOD HOUSEKEEPING

# BEST
# *MICROWAVE*
# RECIPES

GOOD HOUSEKEEPING

# BEST
# *MICROWAVE*
# RECIPES

EBURY PRESS · LONDON

Published by Ebury Press
Division of The National Magazine Company Ltd
Colquhoun House
27–37 Broadwick Street
London W1V 1FR

First impression 1988
Text copyright © 1988 by The National Magazine Company Ltd
Illustrations copyright © 1988 by The National Magazine Company Ltd

ISBN 0 85223 711 1

Edited by Helen Southall
Designed by Bill Mason
Photography by Martin Brigdale, David Johnson,
Paul Kemp, James Murphy.
Illustrations by Angela McAlister

Typeset by Chapterhouse, The Cloisters, Formby L37 3PX
Printed and bound in Spain by Cronion S.A., Barcelona

Dep. Leg. B-28.531-88

# CONTENTS

# GENERAL RECIPE NOTES

Follow either metric or imperial measures for the recipes in this book; they are not interchangeable.

**Egg sizes**
Size 2 eggs should be used unless otherwise stated.

**Bowl sizes**
Small bowl = about 900 ml (1½ pints)
Medium bowl = about 2.3 litres (4 pints)
Large bowl = about 3.4 litres (6 pints)

**Covering**
Cook, uncovered, unless otherwise stated.

At the time of going to press, it has been recommended by the Ministry of Agriculture, Fisheries and Food that the use of cling film should be avoided in microwave cooking. When a recipe requires you to cover the container, either cover with a lid or a plate.

**How to use the recipes in this book with your cooker settings**
Unlike conventional ovens, the power output and heat controls on various microwave cookers do not follow a standard formula. When manufacturers refer to a 700-watt cooker, they are referring to the cooker's POWER OUTPUT; its INPUT, which is indicated on the back of the cooker, is double that figure. The higher the wattage of a cooker, the faster the rate of cooking, thus food cooked at 700 watts on full power cooks in half the time of food cooked at 350 watts. That said, the actual cooking performance of one 700-watt cooker may vary slightly from another with the same wattage because factors such as cooker cavity size affect cooking performance. The vast majority of microwave cookers sold today are either 600, 650 or 700 watts, but there are many cookers still in use which may be 400 and 500 watts.

### IN THIS BOOK
HIGH refers to 100% full power output of 600–700 watts.
MEDIUM refers to 60% of full power.
LOW is 35% of full power.

Whatever the wattage of your cooker, the HIGH/FULL setting will always be 100% of the cooker's output. Thus your highest setting will correspond to HIGH.

However, the MEDIUM and LOW settings used in this book may not be equivalent to the MEDIUM and LOW settings marked on your cooker. As these settings vary according to power input, use the following calculation to estimate the correct setting for a 600–700-watt cooker. This simple calculation should be done before you use the recipes for the first time, to ensure successful results. Multiply the percentage power required by the total number of settings on your cooker and divide by 100. To work out what setting MEDIUM and LOW correspond to on your cooker, use the following calculation.

| Medium (60%) | Low (35%) |
|---|---|
| = %Power required | = %Power required |
| × Total Number | × Total Number |
| of Cooker Settings | of Cooker Settings |
| ÷ 100 = Correct Setting | ÷ 100 = Correct Setting |
| $= \dfrac{60 \times 9}{100} = 5$ | $= \dfrac{35 \times 9}{100} = 3$ |

If your cooker power output is lower than 600 watts, then you must allow a longer cooking and thawing time for all recipes in this book.

Add approximately 10–15 seconds per minute for a 500-watt cooker, and 15–20 seconds per minute for a 400-watt cooker. No matter what the wattage of your cooker is, you should always check food before the end of cooking time, to ensure that it does not get overcooked. Don't forget to allow for standing time.

### Combination Oven Owners
Combination ovens combine conventional and microwave methods of cooking so food browns as well as cooking quickly. One of the disadvantages of cooking in a microwave cooker is that baked dishes do not brown or crisp. In this book, we show you how to overcome these disadvantages. However, if you own a combination oven you will not have these problems. In this case you should follow your oven manufacturer's instructions.

# SOUPS

## CAULIFLOWER SOUP

SERVES 4–6

15 ml (1 tbsp) vegetable oil

1 small onion, skinned and finely chopped

1 small garlic clove, skinned and finely chopped

1 small cauliflower, trimmed

450 ml ($\frac{3}{4}$ pint) boiling vegetable stock

450 ml ($\frac{3}{4}$ pint) milk

freshly grated nutmeg

salt and pepper

snipped fresh chives, to garnish

*1* Put the oil, onion and garlic in a large bowl. Cover and cook on HIGH for 4–5 minutes or until softened, stirring occasionally.

*2* Meanwhile, divide the cauliflower into small florets, discarding the stalks. Add the florets to the bowl with the stock, milk, nutmeg and salt and pepper to taste. Cook on HIGH for 15–20 minutes or until the cauliflower is very tender, stirring occasionally.

*3* Leave to cool slightly, then purée the soup in a blender or food processor.

*4* Pour the soup back into the bowl and reheat on HIGH for 2 minutes or until hot. Ladle the soup into warmed bowls, sprinkle with snipped chives and serve with wholemeal bread, if liked.

## MIXED VEGETABLE SOUP

SERVES 6

1.1 kg (2$\frac{1}{2}$ lb) prepared mixed vegetables such as onions, leeks, carrots, potatoes, swede and celery

2 bay leaves

1 bouquet garni

salt and pepper

150 ml ($\frac{1}{4}$ pint) double cream, crème fraîche, soured cream or single cream (optional)

*1* Finely chop the vegetables and put in a large bowl with the bay leaves, bouquet garni and 1.4 litres (2$\frac{1}{2}$ pints) water.

*2* Cover and cook on HIGH for 30–40 minutes or until the vegetables are very soft. Discard the bouquet garni and bay leaves and purée in a blender or food processor until smooth.

*3* Season to taste with salt and pepper. Return the soup to a clean ovenproof serving bowl and reheat on HIGH for 3–4 minutes or until hot. Stir in cream, if desired.

# SHADES OF GREEN SOUP

### SERVES 4–6

25 g (1 oz) butter or margarine

450 g (1 lb) kale or spring greens, trimmed and chopped

2 leeks, trimmed and sliced

900 ml (1½ pints) boiling vegetable stock

100 g (4 oz) shelled peas or frozen petits pois

½ cos or Webb's wonder lettuce, trimmed

30 ml (2 tbsp) chopped fresh dill

salt and pepper

a few toasted almonds, to garnish

*1* Put the butter, kale and leeks in a large bowl, cover and cook on HIGH for 5–7 minutes or until slightly softened, stirring occasionally.

*2* Add half the stock, re-cover and continue to cook on HIGH for 5–10 minutes or until the vegetables are tender.

*3* Purée the soup in a blender or food processor, then return to the rinsed-out bowl with the remaining stock and the peas. Re-cover and cook on HIGH for 5–7 minutes or until hot.

*4* Meanwhile, finely chop the lettuce. Stir the lettuce and dill into the soup. Season to taste with salt and pepper and serve sprinkled with toasted almonds.

# PASTINA AND SUMMER VEGETABLE SOUP

### SERVES 4

15 ml (1 tbsp) olive oil

100 g (4 oz) new carrots, scrubbed and sliced

100 g (4 oz) French beans, trimmed and cut in half

225 g (8 oz) young peas, shelled

50 g (2 oz) pastina

900 ml (1½ pints) boiling vegetable stock

30 ml (2 tbsp) chopped fresh mint

4 lettuce leaves, finely shredded

salt and pepper

*1* Put the oil, carrots, beans and peas in a large bowl. Cover and cook on HIGH for 2 minutes, stirring once.

*2* Add the pastina and stock. Re-cover and cook on HIGH for 10 minutes or until the pasta and vegetables are tender.

*3* Stir in the mint and lettuce and season with salt and pepper to taste. Cook on HIGH for 1 minute or until the lettuce is just wilted. Serve hot.

*Pastina and Summer Vegetable Soup*

## SPINACH SOUP

### SERVES 4

15 ml (1 tbsp) vegetable oil

1 large onion, skinned and chopped

450 g (1 lb) fresh spinach, trimmed and roughly chopped or 225 g (8 oz) frozen chopped spinach

15 ml (1 level tbsp) plain flour

600 ml (1 pint) boiling chicken or vegetable stock

freshly grated nutmeg

salt and pepper

60 ml (4 tbsp) natural yogurt

*1* Put the oil and onion in a medium bowl. Cover and cook on HIGH for 5–7 minutes or until softened.

*2* Add the spinach, re-cover and cook on HIGH for 3–4 minutes, or 8–9 minutes until thawed if using frozen spinach, stirring occasionally.

*3* Sprinkle in the flour and cook on HIGH for 30 seconds, then gradually stir in the stock. Season with nutmeg and salt and pepper to taste. Cook on HIGH for about 4 minutes or until boiling, stirring occasionally.

*4* Leave the soup to cool slightly, then purée in a blender or food processor. Pour the soup back into the bowl and cook on HIGH for 2 minutes or until boiling. Ladle the soup into warmed bowls and swirl a spoonful of yogurt into each before serving.

## TOMATO AND CARROT SOUP

### SERVES 6

25 g (1 oz) butter or margarine

1 large onion, skinned and finely chopped

1 garlic clove, skinned and crushed

225 g (8 oz) carrots, peeled and finely chopped

450 g (1 lb) ripe tomatoes, skinned and chopped

2 eating apples, peeled, cored and diced

1 bouquet garni

1.1 litres (2 pints) boiling chicken stock

salt and pepper

double cream and snipped chives, to garnish

*1* Place the butter in a large bowl and cook on HIGH for 45 seconds or until melted. Stir in the onion and garlic. Cover and cook on HIGH for 3 minutes or until the onion begins to soften.

*2* Add the carrots, tomatoes, apples, bouquet garni and stock. Season to taste with salt and pepper, re-cover and cook on HIGH for about 20 minutes or until the vegetables are tender.

*3* Discard the bouquet garni and purée the soup in a blender or food processor. Pour the soup back into the bowl and reheat on HIGH for 2 minutes or until hot.

*4* Ladle the soup into warmed bowls and swirl with double cream. Sprinkle with chives and serve.

# POTATO AND ONION SOUP

### SERVES 6

40 g (1½ oz) butter or margarine

1 bunch of spring onions, trimmed and chopped

450 g (1 lb) potatoes, peeled and diced

1 bay leaf

600 ml (1 pint) boiling chicken stock

salt and pepper

150 ml (¼ pint) milk

90 ml (6 tbsp) double cream

strips of spring onion, to garnish

*1* Place the butter in a large serving bowl and cook on HIGH for 45 seconds or until melted. Add the spring onions, cover and cook on HIGH for 5–7 minutes or until soft.

*2* Add the potatoes, bay leaf, stock and salt and pepper to taste and cook on HIGH for 15 minutes or until the vegetables are tender. Discard the bay leaf.

*3* Leave the soup to cool slightly, then purée in a blender or food processor.

*4* Pour the soup back into the bowl, add the milk and reheat on HIGH for 4 minutes. Add the cream and whisk thoroughly. Check seasoning. Garnish with strips of spring onion.

# CREAM OF CELERY SOUP

### SERVES 4

25 g (1 oz) butter or margarine

1 large head of celery, washed, trimmed and thinly sliced

1 medium onion, skinned and chopped

900 ml (1½ pints) boiling chicken stock

300 ml (½ pint) milk

salt and pepper

1 bouquet garni

60 ml (4 tbsp) single cream

chopped celery leaves or parsley, to garnish

*1* Put the butter in a large bowl and cook on HIGH for 45 seconds or until melted. Stir in the celery and onion. Cover and cook on HIGH for 6–8 minutes or until the celery softens, stirring frequently.

*2* Add the stock, milk, salt, pepper and bouquet garni. Re-cover and cook on HIGH for 18–20 minutes or until the celery is very soft.

*3* Cool the soup slightly, remove the bouquet garni and purée in a blender or food processor.

*4* Return the soup to a clean serving bowl and reheat on HIGH for 2 minutes.

*5* Stir the cream into the soup and serve garnished with celery leaves or parsley.

# BARLEY AND CHICK-PEA SOUP

### SERVES 4

15 ml (1 tbsp) olive oil

1 large onion, skinned and chopped

1 garlic clove, skinned and chopped

50 g (2 oz) pot barley

900 ml (1½ pints) boiling vegetable stock

2.5 ml (½ level tsp) ground turmeric

2.5 ml (½ tsp) concentrated mint sauce

100 g (4 oz) fresh spinach, washed, trimmed and shredded

397 g (14 oz) can chick-peas, drained and rinsed

salt and pepper

60 ml (4 tbsp) set natural yogurt (optional)

10 ml (2 level tsp) sesame seeds, toasted (optional)

*1* Put the oil, onion and garlic in a large bowl. Cook on HIGH for 2 minutes, stirring once.

*2* Add the barley, stock, turmeric and concentrated mint sauce. Cover and cook on HIGH for 20 minutes or until the barley is tender, stirring occasionally.

*3* Stir in the spinach and chick-peas and season to taste with salt and pepper. Recover and cook on HIGH for 2–3 minutes or until heated through.

*4* Pour into four soup bowls. Top each bowl with a spoonful of yogurt and sprinkle with sesame seeds if liked. Serve immediately.

# VEGETABLE AND OATMEAL BROTH

### SERVES 4–6

100 g (4 oz) sweetcorn kernels

1 medium onion, skinned and finely chopped

175 g (6 oz) swede, peeled and finely diced

2 medium carrots, peeled and finely diced

1 medium leek, trimmed and sliced

900 ml (1½ pints) boiling vegetable stock

25 g (1 oz) fine oatmeal

45 ml (3 tbsp) chopped fresh parsley

salt and pepper

*1* Put the corn, onion, swede, carrot, leek and 300 ml (½ pint) of the vegetable stock in a large bowl. Cover and cook on HIGH for 12–15 minutes or until the vegetables are tender.

*2* Sprinkle in the oatmeal and stir together. Pour in the remaining vegetable stock and parsley and season to taste with salt and pepper.

*3* Cook on HIGH for 5 minutes or until boiling and thickened, stirring occasionally. Serve the soup hot.

*Barley and Chick-pea Soup*

## SPICY LENTIL SOUP

### SERVES 1

15 ml (1 tbsp) vegetable oil

1 shallot or ½ small onion, skinned and finely chopped

1 medium carrot, peeled and grated

1 small garlic clove, skinned and crushed

pinch of chilli powder

1.25 ml (¼ level tsp) ground cardamom

1.25 ml (¼ level tsp) ground ginger

25 g (1 oz) split red lentils

300 ml (½ pint) boiling chicken stock

75 ml (3 fl oz) milk

salt and pepper

chopped fresh coriander, to garnish

*1* Put the oil, shallot and carrot in a medium bowl, cover and cook on HIGH for 3–4 minutes or until softened, stirring occasionally.

*2* Stir in the garlic, chilli powder, cardamom and ginger and cook on HIGH for 1 minute, stirring once.

*3* Stir in the lentils and three quarters of the stock, re-cover and cook on HIGH for 8–10 minutes or until the lentils are cooked, stirring occasionally.

*4* Allow the soup to cool slightly, then purée in a blender or food processor. Return to the bowl and stir in the remaining stock and the milk. Season to taste with salt and pepper.

*5* Reheat on HIGH for 1–2 minutes or until heated through. Garnish with coriander and serve hot.

## WATERCRESS SOUP

### SERVES 6

50 g (2 oz) butter or margarine, diced

1 large onion, skinned and chopped

2 large bunches of watercress, trimmed, washed and chopped

45 ml (3 level tbsp) plain flour

1.1 litres (2 pints) boiling chicken stock

salt and pepper

150 ml (¼ pint) single cream

watercress sprigs, to garnish

*1* Put the butter in a large bowl and cook on HIGH for 1 minute or until melted. Add the onion, cover and cook on HIGH for 5–7 minutes or until the onion softens.

*2* Add the watercress, re-cover and cook on HIGH for 1–2 minutes. Stir in the flour and cook on HIGH for 30 seconds. Gradually stir in the stock and season to taste with salt and pepper. Re-cover and cook on HIGH for 8 minutes, stirring frequently.

*3* Allow the soup to cool for about 5 minutes, then purée in a blender or food processor until smooth.

*4* Return the soup to a clean bowl and stir in the cream. Reheat on LOW for 6–7 minutes or until hot but not boiling, stirring frequently. Serve either hot or well chilled, garnished with watercress sprigs.

# GREEN SPLIT PEA SOUP

### SERVES 4–6

175 g (6 oz) green split peas

2 leeks, trimmed and finely chopped

2 celery sticks, trimmed and finely chopped

2 medium carrots, peeled and finely chopped

1 garlic clove, skinned and crushed

15 ml (1 tbsp) olive oil

freshly grated nutmeg

salt and pepper

chopped fresh parsley, to garnish

*1* Put the peas in a large bowl and pour over enough water to cover. Leave to soak overnight.

*2* The next day, put the leeks, celery, carrots, garlic and oil in a large bowl. Cover and cook on HIGH for 5 minutes.

*3* Drain the peas and add to the vegetables. Pour in 900 ml (1½ pints) boiling water and mix well together. Re-cover and cook on HIGH for 25 minutes or until the peas are very soft, stirring occasionally.

*4* Purée the soup in a blender or food processor. Season to taste with nutmeg and salt and pepper and pour into an ovenproof serving bowl.

*5* Reheat the soup on HIGH for 3 minutes or until the soup is hot. Garnish with parsley and serve immediately with warm wholemeal or white bread rolls.

# ALMOND SOUP

### SERVES 6

100 g (4 oz) ground almonds

2 celery sticks, trimmed and finely chopped

1 small onion, skinned and finely chopped

600 ml (1 pint) boiling chicken stock

25 g (1 oz) butter or margarine

25 g (1 oz) plain flour

300 ml (½ pint) milk

45 ml (3 tbsp) double cream

1 egg yolk

salt and pepper

toasted flaked almonds, to garnish

*1* Mix the almonds, celery and onion together in a large bowl and pour in the stock. Cover and cook on HIGH for 10 minutes or until boiling, then continue cooking for a further 4 minutes.

*2* Strain the liquid through a sieve and rub the almond paste through using a wooden spoon.

*3* Place the butter in the rinsed-out bowl and cook on HIGH for 45 seconds or until melted. Stir in the flour and cook on HIGH for 30 seconds. Gradually whisk in the milk and almond liquid and cook on HIGH for 3 minutes or until boiling.

*4* Blend the cream and egg yolk together and slowly add to the soup, stirring until well blended. Season to taste with salt and pepper. Garnish with toasted almonds and serve.

## WATERZOOI

### SERVES 6

15 ml (1 tbsp) vegetable oil

2.5 ml ($\frac{1}{2}$ level tsp) ground cloves

2 celery sticks, trimmed and chopped

2 leeks, trimmed and sliced

2 large carrots, peeled and thinly sliced

1 bouquet garni

2 strips of lemon rind

600 ml (1 pint) boiling fish or vegetable stock

700 g (1$\frac{1}{2}$ lb) freshwater fish fillets, such as bream, carp, pike or eel, skinned

salt and pepper

2 egg yolks

150 ml ($\frac{1}{4}$ pint) milk

6 slices of toast

30 ml (2 tbsp) chopped fresh parsley

*1* Put the oil, cloves, celery, leeks, carrots, bouquet garni, lemon rind and half the stock in a large bowl. Cover and cook on HIGH for 12–14 minutes or until the vegetables are softened.

*2* Meanwhile, cut the fish into bite-sized pieces.

*3* Add the fish, remaining stock and salt and pepper to taste to the soup. Re-cover and cook on HIGH for 6–7 minutes until cooked.

*4* Meanwhile, blend the egg yolks and milk together. When the fish is cooked, spoon a little of the liquid on to the egg yolk mixture and mix together. Pour back into the soup.

*5* Re-cover and cook on MEDIUM for 1–2 minutes or until thickened, stirring once; do not allow the soup to boil or it will curdle. Discard the lemon rind and bouquet garni.

*6* To serve, place the toast in six soup bowls, carefully spoon over the soup and garnish with chopped parsley. Serve immediately.

## JAPANESE CLEAR SOUP WITH PRAWNS

### SERVES 4

15 g ($\frac{1}{2}$ oz) dried seaweed, such as kombu, wakame or nori

15 ml (1 tbsp) soy sauce

4 raw jumbo prawns in the shell

2 medium carrots, peeled

5 cm (2 inch) piece of daikon radish, peeled

15 ml (1 tbsp) sake or dry sherry

4 slices of lime

*1* Put the seaweed, soy sauce and 900 ml (1$\frac{1}{2}$ pints) boiling water into a large bowl. Cover and cook on HIGH for 3 minutes or until the water returns to the boil, then continue cooking for a further 5 minutes.

*2* Meanwhile, remove the shells from the prawns, leaving the tail intact. Then, using kitchen scissors or a sharp knife, cut along the curved underside of the prawn from the thick end towards the tail, stopping at the tail and being careful not to cut the prawn through completely.

*3* Flatten out the prawns and remove and discard the veins. Cut a slit in the middle of the prawn, curl the tail round and push it through the slit.

*4* Cut the carrots and daikon radish into thin slices or decorative shapes.

*5* Remove and discard the seaweed from the stock. Stir the sake, carrots and daikon radish into the stock. Cover and cook on HIGH for 3 minutes, then add the prawns and cook for 2 minutes or until cooked.

*6* Using a slotted spoon, transfer the fish and vegetables to four soup bowls, then carefully pour over the stock. Add a slice of lime to each bowl and serve immediately.

*Japanese Clear Soup with Prawns (top); Waterzooi*

## INDONESIAN SOUP

### SERVES 4–6

25 g (1 oz) tamarind

2 garlic cloves, skinned and crushed

5 cm (2 inch) piece of root ginger, peeled and finely grated

1 green chilli, seeded and chopped

5 ml (1 level tsp) ground coriander

15 ml (1 tbsp) vegetable oil

75 g (3 oz) creamed coconut

30 ml (2 tbsp) crunchy peanut butter

1 small squid, cleaned

75 g (3 oz) medium egg noodles

175 g (6 oz) peeled scampi or prawns

75 g (3 oz) firm tofu

5 ml (1 tsp) chopped fresh lemon grass or grated lemon rind

salt and pepper

chopped spring onions, to garnish

1 Put the tamarind and 150 ml ($\frac{1}{4}$ pint) water into a small bowl and leave to soak.

2 Meanwhile, put the garlic, ginger, chilli, coriander and oil into a large bowl and cook on HIGH for 2 minutes, stirring once after 1 minute.

3 Put the coconut and peanut butter into a large jug and pour over 900 ml (1$\frac{1}{2}$ pints) boiling water. Stir until dissolved, then stir into the spice mixture. Cut the squid into small rings and stir into the soup.

4 Cover and cook on HIGH for 5–6 minutes or until boiling. When the soup is boiling, add the noodles and the scampi. Re-cover and cook on HIGH for 3–4 minutes or until the soup just returns to the boil and the noodles are tender, stirring occasionally.

5 Strain the tamarind and water mixture, pressing on the soft pulp to extract the juices. Discard the pulp, then add the brown liquid to the soup.

6 Cut the tofu into 2.5 cm (1 inch) cubes and stir into the soup with the lemon grass and salt and pepper to taste. Reheat on HIGH for 1 minute. Garnish with spring onions, then serve immediately with prawn crackers.

## WALNUT SOUP

### SERVES 4–6

1 garlic clove, skinned

175 g (6 oz) walnuts

600 ml (1 pint) boiling chicken stock

150 ml ($\frac{1}{4}$ pint) single cream

salt and pepper

1 Finely crush the garlic and walnuts together in a blender or food processor. (If using a blender you may need to add a little stock to blend the walnuts.) Very gradually pour in the stock and purée until smooth.

2 Pour the soup into a medium bowl and cook on HIGH for 8–10 minutes or until boiling, stirring occasionally.

3 Stir in the cream, reserving about 60 ml (4 tbsp), and season to taste with salt and pepper. Serve hot, garnished with a swirl of the remaining cream.

# SMOKED HADDOCK CHOWDER

### SERVES 4

1 large onion, skinned

225 g (8 oz) potato, peeled

225 g (8 oz) carrots, peeled

2 celery sticks, trimmed and finely chopped

450 g (1 lb) smoked haddock fillets, skinned

568 ml (1 pint) milk

salt and pepper

15 ml (1 tbsp) lemon juice

*1* Grate the onion, potato and carrots into a large bowl. Add the celery and 150 ml ($\frac{1}{4}$ pint) water, cover and cook on HIGH for 12–14 minutes or until the vegetables are softened.

*2* Meanwhile, cut the fish into 2.5 cm (1 inch) cubes.

*3* Stir the fish into the softened vegetables with the milk, salt and pepper to taste and the lemon juice. Cook on HIGH for 5–6 minutes or until the fish is cooked. Serve immediately.

# THICK PRAWN AND VEGETABLE SOUP

### SERVES 6

15 ml (1 tbsp) olive oil

1 medium onion, skinned and chopped

1 garlic clove, skinned and crushed

5–10 ml (1–2 tsp) sweet chilli sauce (optional)

3 tomatoes, chopped

1 green chilli, seeded and chopped (optional)

5 ml (1 level tsp) dried oregano

1 medium potato, peeled and finely diced

50 g (2 oz) long grain rice

450 ml ($\frac{3}{4}$ pint) milk

75 g (3 oz) frozen petits pois

1 green pepper, seeded and finely chopped

225 g (8 oz) cooked peeled prawns

salt and pepper

*1* Put the oil, onion, garlic, chilli sauce, tomatoes, chilli, oregano, potato, rice and 450 ml ($\frac{3}{4}$ pint) boiling water into a large bowl. Cover and cook on HIGH for 10–12 minutes or until the vegetables are softened, stirring occasionally.

*2* Add the milk, re-cover and cook on HIGH for 10–12 minutes or until the rice is tender.

*3* Add the peas, pepper and prawns and season to taste with salt and pepper. Cover and cook on HIGH for 3–4 minutes. Serve immediately.

## CHINESE STYLE CHICKEN AND BEANSPROUT SOUP

### SERVES 4

1 red pepper, seeded and finely shredded

100 g (4 oz) button mushrooms, thinly sliced

45 ml (3 tbsp) soy sauce

45 ml (3 tbsp) dry sherry

1 cm (½ inch) piece of fresh root ginger, peeled and grated

5 ml (1 tsp) clear honey

100 g (4 oz) cooked chicken breast, skinned

4 spring onions, trimmed

50 g (2 oz) beansprouts

pepper

*1* Put the red pepper in a large bowl with the mushrooms, soy sauce, sherry, ginger, honey and 750 ml (1¼ pints) boiling water. Cook on HIGH for 4–5 minutes or until the pepper is softened.

*2* Meanwhile, thinly shred the chicken and spring onions. Add to the soup with the beansprouts, season to taste with pepper and cook on HIGH for 5 minutes or until heated through, stirring occasionally. Serve hot.

## CHILLED PEA AND MINT SOUP

### SERVES 4–6

50 g (2 oz) butter or margarine

1 medium onion, skinned and roughly chopped

450 g (1 lb) peas

568 ml (1 pint) milk

600 ml (1 pint) boiling chicken stock

2 large fresh mint sprigs

pinch of caster sugar

salt and pepper

150 ml (¼ pint) natural yogurt

mint sprigs, to garnish

*1* Put the butter in a large bowl and cook on HIGH for 45 seconds or until melted.

*2* Add the onion, cover and cook on HIGH for 5–7 minutes, or until the onion is soft.

*3* Add the peas, milk, stock, the two mint sprigs and the sugar. Re-cover and cook on HIGH for about 8 minutes or until boiling. Reduce the setting and continue cooking on LOW for 15 minutes, or until the peas are really tender. Season well with salt and pepper and allow to cool slightly.

*4* Using a slotted spoon, remove about 45 ml (3 tbsp) peas from the soup and put them aside for the garnish. Purée the soup in a blender or food processor until quite smooth.

*5* Pour the soup into a large serving bowl. Adjust the seasoning and leave to cool for 30 minutes. Stir in the yogurt, cover and chill for 2–3 hours before serving.

*6* Serve garnished with the reserved peas and the mint sprigs.

*Chilled Pea and Mint Soup*

# MARBLED ICED BORTSCH

### SERVES 6

1 large onion, skinned and chopped

2 carrots, peeled and chopped

15 ml (1 tbsp) vegetable oil

450 g (1 lb) cooked beetroot, skinned and chopped

1 litre (2 pints) boiling vegetable stock

5 ml (1 level tsp) dark muscovado sugar

15 ml (1 tbsp) lemon juice

### TO SERVE

150 ml ($\frac{1}{4}$ pint) soured cream

salt and pepper

$\frac{1}{2}$ cucumber, chopped

30 ml (2 tbsp) chopped fresh dill

pumpernickel bread

*1* Put the onion, carrot and oil in a large bowl. Cover and cook on HIGH for 5–6 minutes or until slightly softened.

*2* Add the beetroot, stock, sugar and lemon juice, re-cover and cook on HIGH for 10–15 minutes or until the beetroot is very soft, stirring occasionally.

*3* Purée the soup in a blender or food processor. Cover and chill for 3–4 hours or overnight.

*4* To serve, stir in half the cream and season to taste with salt and pepper. Pour into a large bowl or individual serving bowls, then carefully stir in the remaining cream to make a marbled pattern. Mix the cucumber with the dill, and serve separately. Serve the soup with the cucumber and the pumpernickel bread.

# CHILLED BUTTERMILK AND DILL SOUP

### SERVES 1

1 small leek, white part only, trimmed

15 g ($\frac{1}{2}$ oz) butter or margarine

1 medium potato, weighing about 175 g (6 oz), peeled

150 ml ($\frac{1}{4}$ pint) boiling chicken stock

15 ml (1 tbsp) chopped fresh dill

salt and pepper

150 ml ($\frac{1}{4}$ pint) buttermilk

*1* Chop the leek very finely, wash and drain well. Put into a medium bowl with the butter. Grate in the potato, cover and cook on HIGH for 3–4 minutes or until the vegetables have softened, stirring occasionally.

*2* Stir in the chicken stock and half of the dill. Re-cover and cook on HIGH for 5–8 minutes or until the potato is very soft. Season well with salt and pepper.

*3* Allow to cool a little, then purée in a blender or food processor. Pour into a serving bowl and stir in the buttermilk. Chill for at least 2 hours before serving.

*4* To serve, sprinkle the remaining chopped dill on top. Serve the soup with wholemeal bread, if liked.

# VICHYSSOISE

### SERVES 4

50 g (2 oz) butter or margarine

4 leeks, trimmed and sliced

1 medium onion, skinned and sliced

2 potatoes, peeled and sliced

1 litre (1¾ pints) boiling chicken stock

salt and pepper

200 ml (7 fl oz) single cream

fresh chives, to garnish

*1* Cut the butter into cubes and put in a large bowl. Cook on HIGH for 1 minute or until melted. Add the leeks and onion, cover and cook on HIGH for 5–7 minutes or until softened.

*2* Add the potatoes, stock, and salt and pepper to taste and cook on HIGH for 15–17 minutes or until the vegetables are very soft, stirring frequently.

*3* Allow to cool slightly, then purée in a blender or food processor until smooth. Pour into a large serving bowl and stir in the cream. Chill for at least 4 hours.

*4* To serve, whisk the soup to ensure an even consistency. Pour into individual bowls and snip fresh chives on top to garnish.

# CHILLED COURGETTE, MINT AND YOGURT SOUP

### SERVES 4–6

1 medium onion, skinned and finely chopped

1 large potato, peeled and grated

600 ml (1 pint) boiling vegetable stock

450 g (1 lb) courgettes, trimmed and coarsely grated

30 ml (2 tbsp) chopped fresh mint

150 ml (¼ pint) natural yogurt

salt and pepper

courgette slices and mint sprigs, to garnish

*1* Put the onion, potato and half of the stock in a large bowl. Cover and cook on HIGH for 8–10 minutes or until very soft.

*2* Add the courgettes and continue to cook on HIGH for 4 minutes or until the courgettes are soft.

*3* Purée in a blender or food processor. Add the remaining stock, the mint and the yogurt and season to taste with salt and pepper.

*4* Cover and chill in the refrigerator for at least 4 hours before serving garnished with courgette slices and mint sprigs.

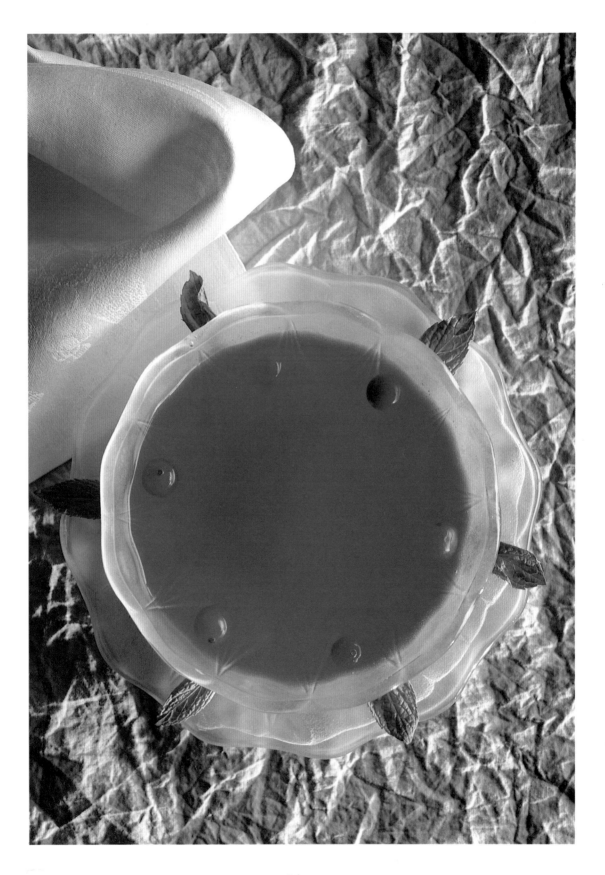

# SPICED CRANBERRY SOUP

### SERVES 4

350 g (12 oz) cranberries

4 whole cloves

1 cinnamon stick

45 ml (3 tbsp) clear honey

15 ml (1 tbsp) Crème de Cassis

a few cranberries and mint leaves, to garnish

*1* Put the cranberries, cloves, cinnamon and honey in a large bowl with 600 ml (1 pint) water. Cover and cook on HIGH for 10–12 minutes or until the cranberries are tender.

*2* Cool slightly then pass the soup through a sieve. Stir in the Crème de Cassis, cover and chill in the refrigerator for at least 4 hours before serving.

*3* To serve, spoon the soup into individual bowls and garnish each with a few cranberries and mint leaves.

# TART APPLE AND GINGER SOUP

### SERVES 4

25 g (1 oz) butter or margarine

2.5 cm (1 inch) piece of fresh root ginger, peeled and grated

large pinch of ground ginger

1 large cooking apple

600 ml (1 pint) boiling vegetable stock

salt and pepper

chopped red apple, to garnish

*1* Put the butter, fresh ginger and ground ginger in a large bowl and cook on HIGH for 2 minutes, stirring once.

*2* Chop the apple roughly (including the peel and core) and add to the ginger with the stock. Cover and cook on HIGH for 10–15 minutes or until the apple is very soft.

*3* Pass the soup through a sieve into a clean bowl and season to taste with salt and pepper. Cover and chill in the refrigerator for at least 4 hours before serving garnished with red apple.

*Spiced Cranberry Soup*

# Starters and Light Meals

## Seafood Scallops

### SERVES 4 AS A STARTER

225 g (8 oz) haddock fillet

150 ml (¼ pint) dry white wine

small piece of onion

1 parsley sprig

1 bay leaf

450 g (1 lb) potatoes, peeled and roughly chopped

75 g (3 oz) butter or margarine

225 ml (8 fl oz) milk

salt and pepper

50 g (2 oz) button mushrooms, thinly sliced

45 ml (3 level tbsp) plain flour

50 g (2 oz) cooked peeled prawns

chopped fresh parsley, to garnish

1 Place the haddock in a shallow dish, pour over the wine and add the onion, parsley and bay leaf. Cover and cook on HIGH for 4–5 minutes or until the fish is tender enough to flake easily.

2 Drain the haddock juices into a measuring jug and make up to 150 ml (¼ pint) with water, if necessary. Skin and flake the fish. Set the fish and the cooking liquid aside.

3 Put the potatoes in a medium bowl and add 175 ml (6 fl oz) water. Cover and cook on HIGH for 6–8 minutes or until the potatoes are cooked, stirring twice. Drain the potatoes well, then mash with 40 g (1½ oz) butter, 25 ml (1 fl oz) milk and salt and pepper to taste. Beat the potatoes until they are smooth and creamy.

4 Put 15 g (½ oz) of the remaining butter in a small bowl and cook on HIGH for 30 seconds or until melted. Stir in the mushrooms, cover and cook on HIGH for 2–3 minutes or until the mushrooms are cooked, shaking the bowl two or three times during cooking.

5 Put the remaining butter in a medium bowl and cook on HIGH for 45 seconds or until melted. Stir in the flour and cook on HIGH for 30 seconds, then gradually whisk in the remaining milk and the reserved fish liquid. Cook on HIGH for 45 seconds, then whisk well. Continue cooking on HIGH for 2 minutes, whisking every 30 seconds until the sauce thickens. Season well with salt and pepper. Stir in the flaked haddock, the mushrooms and the prawns.

6 Spoon the fish mixture into scallop shells or small gratin dishes. Put the potato in a large piping bag fitted with a large star nozzle and pipe a neat potato border around each shell or dish. Cook on HIGH for about 5 minutes or until the scallops are well heated through, re-positioning twice during cooking.

7 Garnish the scallops with parsley and serve immediately. If wished, the scallops may be quickly browned under a hot grill just before serving.

*Seafood Scallops*

# FISH TERRINE WITH TOMATO AND BASIL SAUCE

### SERVES 6 AS A STARTER

16 large basil leaves

700 g (1½ lb) white fish fillets, such as cod, haddock, monkfish or sole, skinned

2 eggs

150 ml (¼ pint) double cream

150 ml (¼ pint) Greek strained yogurt

15 ml (1 tbsp) lemon juice

salt and pepper

4 tomatoes, skinned and seeded

10 ml (2 tsp) tomato purée

*1* Grease a 1.1 litre (2 pint) ring mould and line the base with about 12 of the basil leaves.

*2* Roughly chop the fish and purée in a blender or food processor until smooth. With the machine still running, gradually add 1 egg and the white from the remaining egg, half the cream, half the yogurt and the lemon juice. Season to taste with salt and pepper.

*3* Carefully spoon the fish mixture into the greased mould and level the surface. Cover with a piece of greaseproof paper and cook on MEDIUM for 8–10 minutes or until firm to the touch. Leave to stand for 10 minutes.

*4* Uncover and place a wire rack over the top of the mould. Invert the rack and mould on to a baking tray or shallow dish to catch the liquid that will run out of the mould. Leave to drain for about 5 minutes, then turn over again so that the terrine is still in the mould and the rack is on top. Remove the rack, then unmould the terrine on to a plate. Leave to cool.

*5* To make the sauce, put the tomatoes, remaining cream and yogurt, egg yolk and tomato purée in a blender or food processor and process until smooth. Transfer to a medium bowl and cook on LOW for 3–4 minutes or until slightly thickened, stirring occasionally. Leave to cool.

*6* To serve, cut the terrine into slices and arrange on six serving plates, with a little of the sauce. Finely slice the remaining basil leaves and scatter over the sauce. Serve immediately.

# Warm Salad of Salmon and Scallops

### SERVES 4 AS A LIGHT MEAL

225 g (8 oz) salmon steak or cutlet

8 large shelled scallops

selection of salad leaves, such as curly endive, Webb's wonder lettuce, radicchio and watercress

2 day-old bridge rolls

45 ml (3 tbsp) olive oil

45 ml (3 tbsp) crème fraîche or soured cream

10 ml (2 level tsp) wholegrain mustard

15 ml (1 tbsp) lemon juice

salt and pepper

a few chopped fresh herbs, such as parsley, chives, dill and tarragon

*1* Skin the salmon and remove the bone, if necessary. Cut across the grain into very thin strips. If necessary, remove and discard from each scallop the tough white 'muscle' which is found opposite the coral. Separate the corals from the scallops. Slice the scallops vertically into three or four pieces. Cut the corals in half if they are large.

*2* Heat a browning dish on HIGH for 5–8 minutes or according to manufacturer's instructions.

*3* Meanwhile, tear the salad leaves into small pieces, if necessary, and arrange on four plates. Cut the rolls into thin slices.

*4* Add 30 ml (2 tbsp) of the oil to the browning dish and quickly add the sliced rolls. Cook on HIGH for 2 minutes. Turn over and cook on HIGH for a further 1 minute or until crisp. Remove from the dish and set aside.

*5* Add the remaining oil and the scallops, corals and salmon to the browning dish and cook on HIGH for 1½ minutes or until the fish looks opaque, stirring once.

*6* Using a slotted spoon, remove the fish from the dish, and arrange on top of the salad leaves.

*7* Put the crème fraîche or soured cream, mustard, lemon juice and salt and pepper to taste into the browning dish and cook on HIGH for 1–2 minutes or until hot. Stir thoroughly and pour over the fish. Sprinkle with the bread croûtons and herbs and serve immediately.

# Spicy Prawns

### SERVES 6 AS A STARTER

1 small onion, skinned and finely chopped

1 garlic clove, skinned and chopped

3 large tomatoes, roughly chopped

2.5 cm (1 inch) piece of fresh root ginger, peeled and crushed

2.5 ml (½ level tsp) ground coriander

2.5 ml (½ level tsp) ground cumin

15 ml (1 tbsp) red wine vinegar

5 ml (1 tsp) tomato purée

450 g (1 lb) cooked peeled prawns

salt and pepper

chopped fresh coriander, to garnish

*1* Put the onion, garlic, tomatoes, ginger, coriander, cumin, vinegar and tomato purée in a medium bowl. Cook on HIGH for 10 minutes or until thickened and reduced, stirring occasionally.

*2* Stir in the prawns. Cook on HIGH for 2–3 minutes or until the prawns are heated through, stirring once. Season to taste with salt and pepper. Garnish with chopped coriander and serve hot with poppadums.

## SWEET COOKED CLAMS

### SERVES 2 AS A STARTER

450 g (1 lb) venus clams in the shell

2.5 cm (1 inch) piece of fresh root ginger, peeled and grated

60 ml (4 tbsp) sake or dry sherry

15 ml (1 level tbsp) caster sugar

45 ml (3 tbsp) soy sauce

10 ml (2 level tsp) cornflour

2.5 cm (1 inch) piece of cucumber

1 spring onion, trimmed

*1* Thoroughly scrub the clams.

*2* Put the ginger, sake, sugar and soy sauce in a large bowl and cook on HIGH for 2–3 minutes or until hot. Stir until the sugar is dissolved. Blend the cornflour with 60 ml (4 tbsp) water and stir into the sauce. Cook on HIGH for 2 minutes or until boiling and thickened, stirring once.

*3* Add the clams and stir to coat in the sauce. Cook on HIGH for 4–5 minutes or until the clams have opened, stirring occasionally. Discard any clams which do not open.

*4* Meanwhile, cut the cucumber and onion into very thin strips.

*5* Spoon the clams and sauce on to two plates. Sprinkle with the cucumber and spring onion and serve immediately.

## FRESH PASTA WITH MUSHROOMS

### SERVES 4 AS A LIGHT MEAL

50 g (2 oz) butter or margarine

1 garlic clove, skinned and crushed

450 g (1 lb) button, cup, flat or oyster mushrooms, or a mixture

15 ml (1 tbsp) dry vermouth

150 ml ($\frac{1}{4}$ pint) soured cream

salt and pepper

450 g (1 lb) fresh pasta

chopped fresh herbs, to garnish

*1* Put the butter and garlic in a large bowl and cook on HIGH for 2 minutes, stirring once.

*2* Roughly chop any large mushrooms and stir into the butter with the vermouth. Cover and cook on HIGH for 3–4 minutes or until the mushrooms are just cooked, stirring once. Stir in the cream and season to taste with salt and pepper. Set aside while cooking the pasta.

*3* Put the pasta in a large bowl and pour over enough boiling water to cover by about 2.5 cm (1 inch). Stir once, add salt to taste, then cover and cook on HIGH for 3–4 minutes or until almost tender. Leave to stand, covered, for 5 minutes.

*4* Drain the pasta and mix into the mushroom mixture. Toss lightly together then reheat on HIGH for 1–2 minutes or until hot. Serve immediately garnished with fresh herbs.

*Sweet Cooked Clams*

# PASTA IN SOURED CREAM SAUCE

### SERVES 4 AS A LIGHT MEAL

350 g (12 oz) pasta shapes, such as cartwheels, twists or bows

salt and pepper

10 ml (2 tsp) vegetable oil

100 g (4 oz) butter or margarine

2 shallots, skinned and chopped

30 ml (2 level tbsp) plain flour

150 ml ($\frac{1}{4}$ pint) chicken stock

150 ml ($\frac{1}{4}$ pint) dry white wine

150 ml ($\frac{1}{4}$ pint) soured cream or natural yogurt

100 g (4 oz) button mushrooms, quartered

100 g (4 oz) Cheddar cheese, grated

50 g (2 oz) black olives

200 g (7 oz) can tuna, drained and flaked

chopped fresh parsley, to garnish

*1* Put the pasta in a large bowl and pour over enough boiling water to cover by about 2.5 cm (1 inch). Add 10 ml (2 level tsp) salt and half the vegetable oil.

*2* Stir once, then cover and cook on HIGH for 7 minutes or until almost tender. Leave to stand, covered, for 5 minutes. Drain well.

*3* Put 50 g (2 oz) of the butter in a large serving dish and cook on HIGH for 45 seconds or until melted. Stir in the shallots, cover and cook on HIGH for 4–5 minutes or until the shallots are soft.

*4* Stir the flour into the shallots and cook on HIGH for 1 minute. Gradually stir in the stock and the wine and cook on HIGH for 45 seconds, then whisk well. Continue cooking on HIGH for 2 minutes until the sauce is boiling and thick. Cook for 1 minute more.

*Pasta in Soured Cream Sauce*

5 Stir the soured cream and pasta into the sauce and season to taste with salt and pepper. Add the mushrooms, cheese, olives and tuna and mix gently together.

6 Cover and cook on HIGH for 2 minutes or until hot. Garnish with chopped parsley and serve at once.

## GRANARY BREAD PIZZAS

### SERVES 4 AS A LIGHT MEAL

397 g (14 oz) can chopped tomatoes

15 ml (1 tbsp) tomato purée

1 garlic clove, skinned and crushed

salt and pepper

1 wholemeal or granary bread stick, about 40.5 cm (16 inches) long

50 g (2 oz) mushrooms, thinly sliced

1 medium onion, skinned and thinly sliced

1 green pepper, seeded and cut into thin rings

50 g (2 oz) Mozzarella cheese, grated

5 ml (1 level tsp) dried oregano

1 Put the chopped tomatoes with their juice, tomato purée, garlic and salt and pepper to taste in a medium bowl. Cook on HIGH for 5 minutes or until boiling and slightly reduced.

2 Meanwhile, cut the bread stick in half, then cut each half in half again horizontally to make four pizza bases.

3 Spoon the tomato sauce evenly over the bread and arrange the mushrooms, onion and green pepper on top. Sprinkle with the cheese and oregano.

4 Arrange the pizzas on two serving plates and cook, one plate at a time, on HIGH for 2–3 minutes or until hot. Serve immediately with a green salad.

# FRESH PASTA WITH COURGETTES AND SMOKED TROUT

### SERVES 4 AS A STARTER OR 2 AS A MAIN COURSE

2 medium courgettes

15 ml (1 tbsp) olive oil

pinch of saffron

225 g (8 oz) fresh spinach pasta, such as tagliatelle

salt and pepper

1 smoked trout, weighing about 225 g (8 oz)

150 ml ($\frac{1}{4}$ pint) crème fraîche or double cream

30 ml (2 tbsp) black lumpfish roe

fresh herb sprigs, to garnish

*1* Cut the courgettes into very thin diagonal slices. Cut each slice in half. Put the courgettes, oil and saffron into a medium bowl and cook on HIGH for 1 minute, stirring once.

*2* Put the pasta and salt to taste in a large bowl. Pour over enough boiling water to cover by about 2.5 cm (1 inch), stir once, then cover and cook on HIGH for 3–4 minutes or until almost tender. Leave to stand, covered, while finishing the sauce. Do not drain.

*3* To finish the sauce, remove and discard the skin and bones from the trout. Flake the flesh and stir into the courgettes with the crème fraîche or cream and salt and pepper to taste. Cook on HIGH for 2 minutes or until hot and slightly thickened.

*4* Drain the pasta and return to the large bowl. Pour over the sauce and toss together to mix. If necessary, reheat the sauce and pasta together on HIGH for about 2 minutes. Transfer the pasta to four plates, top each with a spoonful of lumpfish roe and garnish with a herb sprig.

# TAGLIATELLE WITH MUSHROOMS AND TWO CHEESES

### SERVES 2 AS A LIGHT MEAL

225 g (8 oz) fresh tagliatelle

salt and pepper

25 g (1 oz) butter or margarine

1 garlic clove, skinned and crushed

225 g (8 oz) mushrooms, thinly sliced

50 g (2 oz) Stilton cheese

60 ml (4 tbsp) double cream

1 egg, lightly beaten

100 g (4 oz) Mozzarella cheese

*1* Put the tagliatelle and salt to taste in a large bowl and pour over enough boiling water to cover by about 2.5 cm (1 inch). Stir once, then cover and cook on HIGH for 3–4 minutes or until just tender. Leave to stand, covered, for 5 minutes. Do not drain.

*2* Meanwhile, put the butter, garlic and mushrooms in a large bowl, cover and cook on HIGH for 3–4 minutes or until the mushrooms are softened, stirring occasionally. Stir in the Stilton cheese and the cream and cook on HIGH for 2 minutes, stirring once.

*3* Drain the pasta and season with lots of pepper. Mix into the mushroom sauce. Stir in the egg and mix together thoroughly.

*4* Turn the mixture into a buttered flame-proof dish and grate the Mozzarella on top. Cook on HIGH for 3–4 minutes or until heated through. Brown the top under a hot grill before serving with a green salad.

# HAM AND LEEKS AU GRATIN

**SERVES 4 AS A LIGHT MEAL**

8 medium leeks, trimmed and washed

salt and pepper

8 slices of cooked ham

50 g (2 oz) butter or margarine

50 g (2 oz) plain flour

300 ml (½ pint) milk

100 g (4 oz) Gruyère or Cheddar cheese, grated

freshly grated nutmeg

25 g (1 oz) fresh breadcrumbs

chopped fresh parsley, to garnish

*1* Put the leeks in a shallow dish, add 150 ml (¼ pint) water and season with a little salt and pepper. Cover and cook on HIGH for 10–12 minutes or until the leeks are very soft, turning them over and re-positioning them in the dish two or three times during cooking.

*2* Drain the liquid from the leeks into a measuring jug and make up to 300 ml (½ pint) with stock or water, if necessary. Leave the leeks to cool slightly.

*3* When cool enough to handle, wrap each leek in a slice of ham and arrange neatly in a shallow dish.

*4* Put the butter in a small bowl and cook on HIGH for 45 seconds or until melted. Stir in the flour and cook on HIGH for 45 seconds. Gradually whisk in the milk and the reserved cooking liquid. Cook on HIGH for 1 minute, then whisk the mixture thoroughly. Continue to cook on HIGH for about 5 minutes, whisking every 30 seconds until the sauce thickens.

*5* Stir half the cheese into the sauce and then season to taste with salt, pepper and a little grated nutmeg. Continue stirring the sauce until the cheese melts.

*6* Pour the sauce over the leeks and ham and sprinkle with the breadcrumbs and the remaining cheese. Cook on HIGH for 4–5 minutes or until well heated through and the cheese has melted. Garnish with parsley just before serving.

# TAGLIATELLE WITH SMOKED HAM AND PEAS

**SERVES 4 AS A LIGHT MEAL**

225 g (8 oz) dried tagliatelle

salt and pepper

1 medium onion, skinned and thinly sliced

30 ml (2 tbsp) vegetable oil

100 g (4 oz) fresh shelled or frozen peas

225 g (8 oz) piece of smoked ham

150 ml (¼ pint) double cream

50 g (2 oz) freshly grated Parmesan cheese

*1* Place the tagliatelle in a large bowl and pour over enough boiling water to cover by about 2.5 cm (1 inch). Add salt to taste and stir once. Cover and cook on HIGH for 7 minutes or until almost tender. Leave to stand, covered, for 5 minutes. Do not drain.

*2* Mix the onion and oil together in a medium bowl and cook on HIGH for 2 minutes. Stir in the peas, re-cover and cook on HIGH for 5 minutes or until the onion and peas are tender.

*3* Meanwhile, cut the ham into matchstick pieces. Add to the onion and peas along with the cream. Season to taste with salt and pepper and cook on HIGH for 3 minutes or until hot, stirring once or twice.

*4* Drain the tagliatelle and tip into a warmed serving dish. Pour over the sauce and toss lightly. Sprinkle with Parmesan and serve with a mixed salad.

## DEVILLED CHICKEN LIVERS

### SERVES 2 AS A LIGHT MEAL

25 g (1 oz) butter or margarine

1 small onion, skinned and finely chopped

1 garlic clove, skinned and crushed

5 ml (1 level tsp) curry powder

100 g (4 oz) chicken livers, trimmed and cut into bite-sized pieces

pinch of cayenne pepper

salt and pepper

dash of Worcestershire sauce

10 ml (2 tsp) tomato purée

4 thick slices of bread, toasted

*1* Put the butter in a large shallow bowl and cook on HIGH for 45 seconds or until melted. Stir in the onion, garlic and curry powder and cook on HIGH for 3–4 minutes or until slightly softened.

*2* Stir in the chicken livers and cayenne pepper and season to taste with salt and pepper. Stir in the Worcestershire sauce and tomato purée and 15–30 ml (1–2 tbsp) water to make a moist consistency.

*3* Cover and cook on HIGH for 3 minutes or until the livers are just cooked, shaking the bowl occasionally.

*4* Place the toast on two serving plates and spoon the chicken mixture over.

*5* Reheat one plate at a time on HIGH for 30 seconds, then serve immediately.

## KIDNEY AND BACON KEBABS

### SERVES 4 AS A LIGHT MEAL

700 g (1½ lb) lambs' kidneys

8 streaky bacon rashers

100 g (4 oz) button mushrooms

vegetable oil

45 ml (3 tbsp) dry sherry

salt and pepper

*1* Remove the outer membranes from the kidneys and discard. Split each kidney in half lengthways and, using scissors, remove and discard the cores. Prick each kidney half twice with a fork.

*2* Stretch the bacon rashers, using the back of a knife, and cut each in half. Roll up to make 16 bacon rolls.

*3* Thread the kidney halves, bacon and mushrooms on to eight wooden skewers. Arrange on a roasting rack in a single layer, then stand in a large shallow dish. Brush with a little vegetable oil. Cook on HIGH for 8–9 minutes, rearranging and turning once.

*4* Remove the kebabs from the cooker and transfer to a serving dish. Add the sherry to the juices collected in the shallow dish and cook on HIGH for 3–4 minutes or until boiling and slightly reduced. Season to taste with salt and pepper and strain over the kebabs. Serve immediately.

# TINY CHEESE TRIANGLES

## MAKES 12 TRIANGLES

75 g (3 oz) cream, curd or ricotta cheese

15 ml (1 tbsp) lemon or lime juice

*One of more of the following flavourings:*

25 g (1 oz) chopped nuts

30 ml (2 level tbsp) chopped fresh mixed herbs

1 spring onion, trimmed and finely chopped

1 garlic clove, skinned and crushed

25 g (1 oz) chopped dried apricots, dates or figs

a few chopped olives

2.5 cm (1 inch) piece of fresh root ginger, peeled and finely grated

salt and pepper

*For the pastry*

75 g (3 oz) butter or margarine, cut into small pieces

4 sheets of packet filo pastry, each measuring about 45.5 × 28 cm (18 × 11 inches)

*For the sauce (optional)*

75 ml (5 tbsp) natural yogurt

15 ml (1 tbsp) tahini

15 ml (1 tbsp) lemon juice

$\frac{1}{4}$ cucumber

salt and pepper

1 To make the filling, mix the cream cheese and lemon juice with the flavouring of your choice and season to taste with salt and pepper.

2 Put the butter in a small bowl and cook on HIGH for 2 minutes or until melted.

3 Lay one sheet of pastry on top of a second sheet and cut lengthways into six double layer 7.5 cm (3 inch) strips. Repeat with the remaining two strips of pastry.

4 Brush the strips of pastry with the melted butter. Place a generous teaspoonful of filling at one end of each strip. Fold the pastry diagonally across the filling to form a triangle. Continue folding, keeping the triangle shape, until you reach the end of the strip of pastry. Repeat with the remaining strips of pastry to make a total of 12 triangles.

5 Heat a browning dish on HIGH for 5–8 minutes or according to manufacturer's instructions.

6 Meanwhile, brush both sides of each triangle with the melted butter.

7 Using tongs, quickly add six triangles to the dish and cook on HIGH for 1–2 minutes or until the underside of each triangle is golden brown and the top looks puffy. Turn over and cook on HIGH for 1–2 minutes or until the second side is golden brown.

8 Reheat the browning dish on HIGH for 2–3 minutes, then repeat with the remaining triangles.

9 While the filo triangles are cooking, make the sauce, if liked. Put the yogurt, tahini and lemon juice in a bowl and mix together. Grate in the cucumber and season to taste with salt and pepper.

10 Serve the filo triangles warm or cold, with the cucumber and yogurt sauce handed round separately.

MUSH

225 g

1 mediu

1 g

45 r

*1* Put 1
onion
HIGH fo
stirring o

*2* Stir in
minut

*3* Add
(⅓ pin
HIGH fo
tender ar
stirring c
minutes.

*4* Add t
beat
Season t
until cold
the mixt

*5* Divid
triang
minutes.

*6* Heat
5–8
facturer'
and heat

## INDIVIDUAL PASTRY TARTS WITH THREE FILLINGS

### MAKES 4

*For the pastry*

100 g (4 oz) plain wholemeal flour

salt

50 g (2 oz) butter or margarine

45 ml (3 tbsp) chopped fresh mixed herbs

*1* To make the pastry, put the flour and salt to taste in a bowl. Add the butter and rub in until the mixture resembles fine breadcrumbs. Stir in the herbs. Add 30–60 ml (2–4 tbsp) water and knead to a firm, smooth dough.

*2* Roll out the dough thinly. Invert four 10 cm (4 inch) shallow glass flan dishes and cover with the dough. Cover and chill.

*Brie and Watercress Filling*

25 g (1 oz) butter or margarine

2 bunches of watercress

275 g (10 oz) ripe Brie

45 ml (3 tbsp) double cream

freshly grated nutmeg

salt and pepper

Put the butter in a medium bowl and cook on HIGH for 1 minute or until melted. Reserve a few watercress sprigs to garnish and stir the remainder into the butter. Cook on HIGH for 1–2 minutes or until just wilted. Remove the rind from the cheese and cut into small pieces. Stir into the watercress with the cream. Cook on HIGH for 1–2 minutes or until melted. Season to taste with nutmeg, salt and pepper.

*Individual Pastry Tarts with Three Fillings*

*Puréed Mange-tout Filling*

450 g (1 lb) mange-tout, topped and tailed

150 ml (¼ pint) soured cream

salt and pepper

Put the mange-tout and 30 ml (2 tbsp) water in a large bowl. Cover and cook on HIGH for 2 minutes. Remove a few mange-tout and reserve for garnish, then continue to cook the remainder on HIGH for 5–6 minutes or until the mange-tout are really tender, stirring occasionally. Cool slightly, then purée in a blender or food processor with the cream. Season to taste with salt and pepper.

*Creamy Leek and Parmesan Filling*

700 g (1½ lb) leeks, finely sliced

25 g (1 oz) butter or margarine

60 ml (4 tbsp) freshly grated Parmesan cheese

150 ml (¼ pint) double cream

salt and pepper

Reserve a few of the green slices of leek for garnish, then put the remainder in a medium bowl with the butter. Cover and cook on HIGH for 8–10 minutes or until really soft, stirring occasionally. Add the remaining ingredients and cook on HIGH for 1–2 minutes or until hot.

*1* To cook the tarts, uncover and prick all over with a fork. Arrange pastry side uppermost in a circle in the cooker and cook on HIGH for 2–3 minutes or until firm to the touch.

*2* Leave to stand for 5 minutes, then carefully loosen around the edge and invert on to a large serving plate.

*3* Fill with your chosen filling and cook on high for 2–3 minutes or until warmed through. Garnish appropriately with leeks, watercress or mange-tout.

## VEGETARIAN BURGERS

### MAKES 6

2 medium potatoes, each weighing about 175 g (6 oz)

15 ml (1 level tbsp) coriander seeds

5 ml (1 level tsp) cumin seeds

30 ml (2 tbsp) vegetable oil

5 ml (1 level tsp) ground turmeric

1 garlic clove, skinned and crushed

100 g (4 oz) chopped mixed nuts

100 g (4 oz) Cheddar cheese, grated

1 egg yolk

30 ml (2 tbsp) chopped fresh coriander

salt and pepper

*1* Scrub the potatoes and prick them all over with a fork. Cook on HIGH for 8 minutes or until tender, turning over once.

*2* Meanwhile, crush the coriander and cumin in a pestle and mortar.

*3* When the potato is cooked, remove from the cooker and set aside to cool slightly. Put half the oil, the crushed spices, turmeric and garlic in a medium bowl and cook on HIGH for 2 minutes, stirring once.

*4* Peel the potatoes and add to the spices, with the nuts, cheese, egg yolk, coriander and salt and pepper to taste. Mash thoroughly together.

*5* Heat a browning dish on HIGH for 5–8 minutes or according to the manufacturer's instructions.

*6* Meanwhile, using lightly floured hands, shape the mixture into six burgers.

*7* Add the remaining oil to the hot browning dish, then quickly add the burgers. Cook on HIGH for 2 minutes or until browned, then turn over and cook on HIGH for a further 2 minutes. Serve hot.

## AVOCADO, PRAWN AND POTATO SALAD

### SERVES 4 AS A STARTER

350 g (12 oz) small new potatoes, scrubbed and quartered

1 small ripe avocado

150 ml ($\frac{1}{4}$ pint) natural yogurt

15 ml (1 tbsp) lemon juice

5 ml (1 level tsp) wholegrain mustard

salt and pepper

225 g (8 oz) cooked peeled prawns

4 large radishes, trimmed and thinly sliced

2 spring onions, trimmed and thinly sliced

a few lettuce leaves, to garnish

*1* Put the potatoes in a medium bowl with 30 ml (2 tbsp) water. Cover and cook on HIGH for 7–8 minutes or until tender, stirring occasionally.

*2* Meanwhile, cut the avocado in half and remove the stone. Peel. Mash half the flesh with the yogurt, lemon juice, mustard and salt and pepper to taste.

*3* Pour the dressing over the potatoes and toss together with the prawns. Cut the remaining avocado into cubes and mix into the salad with the radishes and spring onions.

*4* Serve while still slightly warm, garnished with a few lettuce leaves.

*Avocado, Prawn and Potato Salad*

# STUFFED PASTA SHELLS WITH A TOMATO VINAIGRETTE

### SERVES 4 AS A LIGHT MEAL

20 large dried pasta shells

salt and pepper

900 g (2 lb) fresh spinach, washed, trimmed and chopped, or a 226 g (8 oz) packet frozen chopped spinach

450 g (1 lb) ricotta cheese

freshly grated nutmeg, ground mixed spice or ground mace

fresh herbs, to garnish

*For the Tomato Vinaigrette*

150 ml ($\frac{1}{4}$ pint) olive oil

30 ml (2 tbsp) lemon juice

10 ml (2 tsp) tomato purée

salt and pepper

*1* Put the pasta shells in a large bowl with salt to taste and pour over enough boiling water to cover by about 2.5 cm (1 inch). Stir once, then cover and cook on H I G H for 18–20 minutes or until almost tender, stirring once during cooking. Leave to stand, covered, for 5 minutes.

*2* Drain the pasta and rinse in cold water. Leave to drain again.

*3* If using fresh spinach, put it in a large bowl, cover and cook on H I G H for 3–4 minutes or until just cooked. If using frozen spinach, cook on H I G H for 8–9 minutes or until thawed. Drain and return to the bowl.

*4* Stir in the ricotta cheese and mix thoroughly together. Season to taste with nutmeg, mixed spice or mace and salt and pepper.

*5* Use the spinach and cheese mixture to stuff the pasta shells and arrange upright on a serving dish.

*6* To make the tomato vinaigrette, whisk the ingredients together and season to taste with salt and pepper. Drizzle over the pasta shells and serve immediately garnished with fresh herbs.

# PIPERADE

### SERVES 2 AS A LIGHT MEAL

4 ripe tomatoes

25 g (1 oz) butter or margarine

1 small green pepper, seeded and chopped

1 garlic clove, skinned and crushed

1 small onion, skinned and finely chopped

salt and pepper

4 eggs, beaten

French bread, to serve

*1* Prick the tomatoes with a fork and cook on HIGH for 1½ minutes or until the skins burst. Peel off the skins, discard the seeds and roughly chop the flesh.

*2* Put the butter in a medium bowl and cook on HIGH for 45 seconds or until melted. Stir in the pepper, garlic and onion.

*3* Cover and cook on HIGH for 3–4 minutes or until softened, stirring occasionally. Season to taste with salt and pepper and stir in the tomatoes. Cook on HIGH for 1 minute, then stir in the eggs.

*4* Cook on HIGH for 2–3 minutes or until the eggs are lightly scrambled, stirring frequently. Serve immediately with French bread and butter.

*Stuffed Pasta Shells with a Tomato Vinaigrette*

## SALADE NIÇOISE

### SERVES 4–6 AS A LIGHT MEAL

175 g (6 oz) small French beans

1 tuna steak, weighing about 275 g (10 oz)

45 ml (3 tbsp) olive oil

4 fresh sardines, scaled and cleaned (optional)

225 g (8 oz) ripe tomatoes

4 hard-boiled eggs

1 large crisp lettuce such as cos, Webb's wonder, batavia, radicchio

100 g (4 oz) black olives

50 g (2 oz) can anchovy fillets in olive oil

15 ml (1 tbsp) lemon juice

salt and pepper

*1* Top and tail the beans and put into a large shallow dish with 15 ml (1 tbsp) water. Cover and cook on HIGH for 2–3 minutes or until slightly softened, stirring once. Drain, rinse with cold water and put in a salad bowl.

*2* Put the tuna into the shallow dish. Brush with some of the olive oil, cover and cook on HIGH for 3 minutes. Meanwhile, remove and discard the heads from the sardines. Cut the fish in half and arrange around the edge of the tuna. Brush with olive oil. Cook the tuna and sardines on HIGH for 1–2 minutes or until tender.

*3* Remove and discard the skin and bones from the tuna, flake the flesh and put into the salad bowl with the beans and sardines. Leave to cool.

*4* When the fish and beans are cold, quarter the tomatoes and hard-boiled eggs and tear the lettuce into large pieces. Add the tomatoes, eggs, lettuce and olives to the salad bowl and carefully mix everything together.

*5* Drain the anchovy fillets, reserving the oil, and mix into the salad. Whisk together the anchovy oil, remaining olive oil, lemon juice and salt and pepper to taste. Pour over the salad and toss together. Serve immediately.

## TUNA, FLAGEOLET AND PASTA SALAD

### SERVES 4 AS A LIGHT MEAL

100 g (4 oz) dried pasta shells

salt and pepper

1 small onion

200 g (7 oz) can tuna in oil

260 g (9½ oz) can flageolet beans

60 ml (4 tbsp) olive oil

30 ml (2 tbsp) lemon juice

black olives

chopped mixed fresh herbs

*1* Put the pasta and salt to taste in a large bowl. Pour over enough boiling water to cover by about 2.5 cm (1 inch). Stir once, cover and cook on HIGH for 6–8 minutes or until just tender, stirring occasionally. Leave to stand, covered, for 5 minutes.

*2* Meanwhile, skin and very thinly slice the onion. Drain and flake the tuna. Drain the beans and rinse.

*3* Drain the cooked pasta, rinse under cold water and drain well. In a salad bowl, toss the pasta with the onion, tuna, beans, oil, lemon juice, black olives, pepper to taste and chopped fresh herbs.

# SPINACH, MUSSEL AND MUSHROOM SALAD

### SERVES 4 AS A STARTER

1 large yellow or red pepper

45 ml (3 tbsp) olive oil

1 small onion, skinned and finely chopped

4 large flat black mushrooms, sliced

700 g (1½ lb) mussels, cleaned

150 ml (¼ pint) dry white wine

salt and pepper

175 g (6 oz) fresh spinach, washed and trimmed

*1* Prick the pepper all over with a fork and rub with a little of the oil. Lay on a piece of absorbent kitchen paper and cook on HIGH for 3–4 minutes or until just soft, turning over once.

*2* Leave to cool slightly, then cut the flesh into neat cubes, discarding the seeds and the core.

*3* Put the remaining oil, onion and mushrooms in a large bowl. Cover and cook on HIGH for 3–4 minutes or until the mushrooms are cooked, stirring once. Using a slotted spoon, remove the mushrooms and add to the cubes of pepper.

*4* Add the mussels and wine to the onion and oil. Cover and cook on HIGH for 3–5 minutes or until all the mussels have opened, removing the mussels on the top as they open and shaking the bowl occasionally. Discard any mussels which do not open.

*5* Drain the mussels in a sieve, reserving the liquid, and mix with the mushrooms and pepper. Return the cooking liquid to the bowl and cook, uncovered, on HIGH for 8–10 minutes or until reduced by half.

*6* Leave the cooking liquid to cool. Season to taste with salt and pepper, then pour over the mussels, mushrooms and peppers and mix all together.

*7* Tear any large spinach leaves into two or three pieces and arrange on four plates. Pour over the mussel mixture and toss lightly together. Serve at once.

# BEAN AND OLIVE PÂTÉ

### SERVES 4–6 AS A STARTER

100 g (4 oz) black-eye beans

175 g (6 oz) black olives, stoned

1 garlic clove, skinned

30 ml (2 tbsp) natural yogurt

15 ml (1 tbsp) lemon juice

15 ml (1 tbsp) olive oil

large pinch of ground cumin

salt and pepper

black olives, to garnish

*1* Put the beans in a large bowl and pour over enough water to cover. Leave to soak overnight.

*2* The next day, drain the beans, return to the bowl and pour over enough boiling water to cover by about 2.5 cm (1 inch). Cover and cook on HIGH for 30–40 minutes or until really tender.

*3* Drain the beans and purée in a blender or food processor with the remaining ingredients.

*4* Turn the purée into a serving bowl and leave to cool. Serve garnished with a few black olives.

## CHICKEN LIVER AND GREEN PEPPERCORN PÂTÉ

SERVES 6 AS A STARTER OR LIGHT MEAL

225 g (8 oz) chicken livers, finely chopped

100 g (4 oz) streaky bacon, rinded and finely chopped

1 medium onion, skinned and finely chopped

15 ml (1 level tbsp) wholegrain mustard

15 ml (1 tbsp) brandy or sherry

1 garlic clove, skinned and crushed

10 ml (2 tsp) green peppercorns, crushed

salt and pepper

100 g (4 oz) butter

lemon slices and parsley sprigs, to garnish

*1* Put the liver, bacon and onion in a large bowl with the mustard, brandy, garlic, green peppercorns and salt and pepper to taste.

*2* Cover and cook on HIGH for 8 minutes, or until the liver and bacon are tender, stirring frequently. Leave to cool.

*3* Purée the pâté mixture in a blender or food processor with the butter. Adjust the seasoning.

*4* Spoon into a serving dish, cover and chill in the refrigerator before serving garnished with lemon slices and parsley sprigs.

## AUBERGINE AND YOGURT PURÉE

SERVES 4 AS A STARTER

1 aubergine, weighing about 450 g (1 lb)

5 ml (1 tsp) vegetable oil

1–2 garlic cloves, skinned and crushed

6 black olives, stoned and roughly chopped

juice of ½ lemon

150 ml (¼ pint) natural yogurt

*1* Rub the aubergine with the oil and prick well all over with a fork. Place on absorbent kitchen paper and cook on HIGH for 8 minutes or until tender, turning over once during cooking.

*2* Leave the aubergine to stand for 5 minutes, then chop roughly, discarding the stalk. Purée in a blender or food processor with the remaining ingredients.

*3* Turn the purée into a bowl and leave to cool. Serve with wholemeal pitta bread, toast or crudités.

*Aubergine and Yogurt Purée*

# CHILLED COURGETTE MOUSSES WITH SAFFRON SAUCE

SERVES 2 AS A STARTER

275 g (10 oz) small courgettes, trimmed

15 g ($\frac{1}{2}$ oz) butter or margarine

7.5 ml (1$\frac{1}{2}$ tsp) lemon juice

100 g (4 oz) low-fat soft cheese

salt and pepper

5 ml (1 level tsp) gelatine

45 ml (3 tbsp) natural yogurt

pinch of saffron strands

1 egg yolk

fresh herb sprigs, to garnish

1 Using a potato peeler or sharp knife, cut one of the courgettes lengthways into very thin strips. Put the slices in a medium bowl with 30 ml (2 tbsp) water, cover and cook on HIGH for 2–3 minutes or until just tender, stirring once. Drain and dry with absorbent kitchen paper.

2 Use the courgette slices to line two oiled 150 ml ($\frac{1}{4}$ pint) ramekin dishes. Set aside while making the filling.

3 Finely chop the remaining courgettes and put in a medium bowl with half the butter and the lemon juice. Cover and cook on HIGH for 5–6 minutes or until tender, stirring occasionally.

4 Allow to cool slightly, then purée in a blender or food processor with the remaining butter and the cheese. Season to taste.

5 Put the gelatine and 15 ml (1 tbsp) water in a small bowl or cup and cook on LOW for 1–1$\frac{1}{2}$ minutes or until the gelatine has dissolved, stirring occasionally. Add to the courgette purée and mix together thoroughly. Pour into the lined dishes and leave to cool. Chill for at least 1 hour or until set.

6 Meanwhile, make the sauce. Put the yogurt, saffron, egg yolk and salt and pepper to taste in a small bowl and cook on LOW for 1–1$\frac{1}{2}$ minutes or until slightly thickened, stirring frequently. Strain, then leave to cool.

7 To serve, loosen the courgette moulds with a palette knife, then turn out on to two individual serving plates. Pour over the sauce, garnish with a fresh herb sprig and serve immediately.

# RAMEKINS OF SMOKED TROUT

SERVES 4 AS A STARTER

one 250 g (9 oz) smoked trout

150 g (5 oz) low-fat soft cheese

45 ml (3 tbsp) natural yogurt

15 ml (1 level tbsp) horseradish sauce

2 egg yolks

pepper

1 egg white

1 Flake the fish, discarding the skin and bones, and put in a bowl. Add the cheese, yogurt, horseradish, egg yolks and pepper to taste and beat together.

2 Whisk the egg white until stiff but not dry, then fold into the fish mixture.

3 Spoon the mixture into four 150 ml ($\frac{1}{4}$ pint) ramekin dishes. Cook on HIGH for 4 minutes or until lightly set. Serve with wholemeal bread.

# SMOKED FISH PÂTÉ

### SERVES 4 AS A STARTER

350 g (12 oz) smoked haddock fillet

1 small lemon

75 g (3 oz) butter or margarine

5 ml (1 tsp) snipped chives

pepper

*1* Place the fish in a shallow dish with 60 ml (4 tbsp) water. Cover and cook on HIGH for 6 minutes or until tender. Drain well. Remove the skin and flake the fish, discarding any bones.

*2* Cut four slices from the lemon. Finely grate the rind and squeeze the juice from the remaining lemon.

*3* Place the butter in a medium bowl and cook on HIGH for 45 seconds or until melted. Stir in the flaked haddock, lemon rind, lemon juice and chives. Season to taste with pepper and mix well together.

*4* Divide the pâté equally between four ramekin dishes. Cover and chill in the refrigerator for at least 4 hours. Garnish with the lemon slices and serve with Melba toast or hot buttered toast.

# CIDER-SOUSED MACKEREL

### SERVES 4 AS A STARTER OR LIGHT MEAL

4 mackerel or herrings, each weighing about 275 g (10 oz), cleaned

salt and pepper

1 medium onion, skinned and very thinly sliced

150 ml ($\frac{1}{4}$ pint) dry cider

45 ml (3 tbsp) cider or white wine vinegar

3 black peppercorns

2 allspice berries

2 cloves

2 bay leaves

$\frac{1}{2}$ lemon, thinly sliced

*1* Fillet the fish, leaving the tails attached. Season the fillets to taste with salt and pepper, then roll up each fillet towards the tail with the flesh side inside. Secure with cocktail sticks.

*2* Arrange the fish around the edge of a shallow dish with the tails pointing upwards.

*3* Scatter the onion slices on top of the fish. Pour over the cider and vinegar and sprinkle with the remaining ingredients.

*4* Cover and cook on HIGH for 7–8 minutes or until the fish is tender, basting occasionally. Leave to cool in the dish, basting occasionally with the cooking liquid.

# FISH MAIN DISHES

## FISH WITH CORIANDER MASALA

### SERVES 2–3

1 medium onion, skinned and chopped

2 garlic cloves, skinned

1 green chilli, seeded (optional)

2.5 cm (1 inch) piece of fresh root ginger, peeled

15 ml (1 level tbsp) coriander seeds

5 ml (1 level tsp) ground turmeric

5 ml (1 level tsp) fenugreek seeds

45 ml (3 tbsp) chopped fresh coriander

juice of 2 limes

30 ml (2 tbsp) vegetable oil

4 large tomatoes, finely chopped

15 ml (1 level tbsp) garam masala

salt

1 whole fish, such as whiting, codling or pollack, weighing about 700–900 g (1½–2 lb), scaled and cleaned

fresh coriander and lime slices, to garnish

1 Put the onion, garlic, chilli, ginger, coriander seeds, turmeric, fenugreek seeds, fresh coriander and lime juice in a blender or food processor and process until smooth.

2 Put the oil in a large shallow dish (large enough to hold the fish) and cook on H I G H for 1 minute or until hot. Add the spice paste and cook on H I G H for 5 minutes, or until the onion is softened, stirring occasionally.

3 Add the tomatoes, garam masala and salt to taste and cook on H I G H for 3–4 minutes or until the sauce is reduced and slightly thickened, stirring occasionally.

4 Meanwhile, using a sharp knife, make deep cuts in a criss-cross pattern on each side of the fish. If the fish is too large for the microwave, push a long bamboo skewer through the tail and then into the body of the fish so that the tail is curved upwards.

5 Lay the fish in the dish containing the sauce and spoon the sauce over the fish to coat it. Cover and cook on H I G H for 10–15 minutes, depending on the thickness of the fish, or until the fish is tender. Serve garnished with coriander and lime.

*Fish with Coriander Masala*

## SOLE AND SPINACH ROULADES

### SERVES 4

12 sole fillets, each weighing about 75 g (3 oz), skinned

5 ml (1 level tsp) fennel seeds, lightly crushed

salt and pepper

12 spinach or sorrel leaves, washed

15 ml (1 tbsp) dry white wine

45 ml (3 tbsp) Greek strained yogurt

pinch of ground turmeric

*1* Place the sole fillets, skinned side up, on a chopping board. Sprinkle with the fennel seeds and season to taste with salt and pepper. Lay a spinach or sorrel leaf, vein side up, on top of each fillet, then roll up and secure with a wooden cocktail stick.

*2* Arrange the fish in a circle around the edge of a large shallow dish and pour over the wine. Cover and cook on HIGH for 6–7 minutes or until tender.

*3* Remove the fish from the cooking liquid, using a slotted spoon, and transfer to a serving plate.

*4* Gradually stir the yogurt and turmeric into the cooking liquid. Season to taste with salt and pepper and cook on HIGH for 1–2 minutes or until slightly thickened, stirring occasionally. Serve the roulades with a little of the sauce poured over.

## FISH STEAKS WITH HAZELNUT SAUCE

### SERVES 4

100 g (4 oz) hazelnuts

4 white fish steaks, such as haddock or cod, each weighing about 175 g (6 oz)

45 ml (3 tbsp) dry white wine, or fish or vegetable stock

150 ml ($\frac{1}{4}$ pint) double cream or Greek strained yogurt

salt and pepper

ground mace

watercress sprigs, to garnish

*1* Spread the hazelnuts out on a large plate and cook on HIGH for 30 seconds. Tip on to a clean tea-towel and rub off the loose brown skin. Return the nuts to the cooker and cook on HIGH for 6–10 minutes, stirring frequently, until lightly browned. Chop finely.

*2* Arrange the fish in a single layer in a large shallow dish and pour over the wine or stock. Cover and cook on HIGH for 6–7 minutes or until the fish is cooked. Transfer the fish to a serving dish.

*3* Add the hazelnuts and cream or yogurt to the cooking dish and cook on HIGH for 2 minutes or until hot. Season to taste with salt, pepper and mace, then pour over the fish. Garnish with watercress sprigs and serve immediately.

# COD WITH WATERCRESS SAUCE

### SERVES 2

1 small bunch of watercress

30 ml (2 tbsp) natural yogurt

5 ml (1 tsp) lemon juice

5 ml (1 level tsp) mild mustard

1 egg yolk

salt and pepper

75 ml (5 tbsp) vegetable oil

2 cod steaks, each weighing about 175 g (6 oz)

15 ml (1 level tbsp) plain flour

15 g ($\frac{1}{2}$ oz) butter or margarine

*1* Wash and trim the watercress. Reserve a few sprigs for garnish, then put the rest in a large bowl with 15 ml (1 tbsp) water. Cover and cook on HIGH for 1 minute or until the watercress looks slightly limp.

*2* Drain the watercress and let it cool a little, then purée in a blender or food processor with the yogurt. Set aside.

*3* Heat a browning dish on HIGH for 5–8 minutes or according to manufacturer's instructions.

*4* Meanwhile, put half the lemon juice, the mustard, egg yolk and salt and pepper to taste in a medium bowl. Whisk together, then gradually whisk in the oil, a little at a time, until the mixture becomes thick and creamy.

*5* When all the oil has been added, add the remaining lemon juice and more seasoning if necessary. Fold in the watercress purée and set aside.

*6* Lightly coat the fish with the flour and season to taste with salt and pepper. Put the butter in the browning dish, then quickly add the fish. Cook on HIGH for 2 minutes, then turn over and cook on HIGH for 1–2 minutes or until tender. Transfer to two plates.

*7* Cook the watercress sauce on HIGH for 1 minute or until warm, stirring occasionally. Pour over the fish, garnish with the reserved watercress sprigs and serve immediately.

# RED MULLET WITH HOT RED PEPPER SAUCE

### SERVES 4

1 large red pepper

7.5 ml (1$\frac{1}{2}$ tsp) sweet chilli sauce

75 ml (5 tbsp) vegetable stock

salt and pepper

4 red mullet, each weighing about 175 g (6 oz), cleaned and scaled

lemon or lime wedges, to garnish

*1* Place the pepper in a large bowl with 30 ml (2 tbsp) water. Cover and cook on HIGH for 10–12 minutes or until very soft.

*2* Plunge the pepper into cold water for 1 minute. Drain well, remove the seeds and peel off the skin.

*3* Purée the pepper in a blender or food processor with the chilli sauce and stock. Season to taste with salt and pepper.

*4* Slash the fish on each side using a sharp knife, and arrange in a large shallow dish. Add 45 ml (3 tbsp) water. Cover and cook on HIGH for 4–5 minutes or until tender, turning the fish over halfway through cooking. Allow to stand while reheating the sauce.

*5* Put the sauce in a medium bowl. Cover and cook on HIGH for 1–2 minutes or until heated through.

*6* To serve, place the fish on four warmed serving plates and spoon over the sauce. Garnish with lemon or lime wedges.

# PARCHMENT BAKED SALMON WITH CUCUMBER SAUCE

### SERVES 2

25 g (1 oz) butter or margarine

½ small cucumber, thinly sliced

2 spring onions, finely chopped

60 ml (4 tbsp) dry white wine

10 ml (2 tsp) chopped fresh dill

1.25 ml (¼ level tsp) fennel seeds

salt and pepper

2 salmon steaks, weighing about 175 g (6 oz) each

45 ml (3 tbsp) mayonnaise

30 ml (2 tbsp) natural yogurt

1.25 ml (¼ tsp) lemon juice

fresh dill, to garnish

*1* Put half the butter in a small bowl and cook on HIGH for 30 seconds or until melted. Stir in the cucumber slices, reserving six for cooking the salmon, and the spring onions.

*2* Cover and cook on HIGH for 4–5 minutes or until tender. Stir in half the wine and half the fresh dill, and cook, uncovered, on HIGH for 2 minutes. Leave to cool.

*3* Meanwhile, put the remaining butter, the fennel seeds and the remaining wine in a small bowl and cook on HIGH for 2 minutes or until reduced by half. Season to taste with salt and pepper.

*4* Cut two 28 cm (11 inch) squares of non-stick parchment or greaseproof paper and place a salmon steak on each. Arrange the reserved cucumber slices on top and pour over the butter, wine and fennel seeds. Fold the paper to make two neat parcels.

*Parchment Baked Salmon with Cucumber Sauce*

*5* Place the parcels on a plate and microwave on HIGH for 4–5 minutes or until the fish is tender.

*6* While the fish is cooking, finish the sauce. Purée the cooled cucumber and onion mixture in a blender or food processor with the mayonnaise, yogurt, lemon juice, remaining dill, salt and pepper.

*7* Garnish the salmon with dill and serve warm with the cucumber sauce.

# BAKED RED MULLET EN PAPILLOTE

### SERVES 2

2 red mullet, each weighing about 175 g (6 oz), cleaned and scaled

salt and pepper

½ small onion, skinned and thinly sliced

2 parsley sprigs

2 bay leaves

2 lemon slices

*1* Slash the fish on each side using a sharp knife. Season the insides with salt and pepper to taste. Use the onion, parsley, bay leaves and lemon slices to stuff the fish.

*2* Cut two 30.5 cm (12 inch) squares of greaseproof paper. Place a fish on each piece and fold it to make a neat parcel, twisting the ends together to seal. Place on a large flat plate.

*3* Cook on HIGH for 3–4 minutes or until the fish is tender. Serve the fish in their parcels.

## SEA BASS COOKED WITH A SPICE PASTE

### SERVES 6

1 green chilli, seeded and chopped

2 garlic cloves, skinned and crushed

30 ml (2 level tbsp) desiccated coconut

45 ml (3 level tbsp) ground almonds

45 ml (3 tbsp) chopped fresh coriander

2.5 cm (1 inch) piece of fresh root ginger, peeled and grated

10 ml (2 level tsp) ground cumin

5 ml (1 level tsp) ground cardamom

5 ml (1 level tsp) ground mixed spice

finely grated rind and juice of 1 lime

salt and pepper

1 sea bass, weighing about 1.5 kg (3½ lb), cleaned and scaled

30 ml (2 tbsp) olive oil

lime slices and fresh coriander, to garnish

*1* Put the chilli, garlic, coconut, almonds, coriander, ginger, cumin, cardamom, mixed spice and lime rind and juice in a blender or food processor with 150 ml (¼ pint) water and purée until smooth. Season to taste with salt and pepper.

*2* Using a sharp knife, remove and discard the head and tail from the fish, then make four or five deep cuts on each side of the fish. Spread the spice paste into the cuts and all over the fish.

*3* Put the fish in a shallow dish and pour over the oil. Cover and cook on H I G H for about 13–15 minutes or until the fish is tender and looks opaque. Leave to stand for 5 minutes.

*4* Serve garnished with lime slices and fresh coriander sprigs.

## MACKEREL WITH CITRUS FRUIT

### SERVES 4

1 medium orange

1 lemon

1 lime

4 mackerel, each weighing about 350 g (12 oz), cleaned

salt and pepper

chopped fresh parsley, to garnish

*1* Using a potato peeler or a very sharp knife, peel the rind from the orange, lemon and lime. Remove and discard any white pith from the rind.

*2* Cut the rind into fine shreds and put in a large shallow dish. Squeeze the juice from the fruits into the dish.

*3* Cook on H I G H for 3–4 minutes or until the rind is slightly softened, stirring occasionally.

*4* Remove and discard the heads from the fish, then slash the skin twice on each side using a sharp knife. Arrange the fish in the dish with the citrus rind, cover and cook on H I G H for about 10 minutes or until the fish is tender, rearranging the fish once during cooking. Season to taste with salt and pepper and serve immediately garnished with chopped parsley.

# FISH MOUSSAKA

## SERVES 4–6

2 aubergines, each weighing about 225 g (8 oz)

15 ml (1 tbsp) vegetable oil

1 medium onion, skinned and finely chopped

1 garlic clove, skinned and crushed

5 ml (1 level tsp) ground cinnamon

5 ml (1 level tsp) dried oregano

397 g (14 oz) can tomatoes

15 ml (1 tbsp) tomato purée

700 g (1½ lb) oily fish fillets, such as mackerel, herring or pilchard, skinned

salt and pepper

2 eggs, beaten

300 ml (½ pint) natural yogurt

freshly grated nutmeg

15 g (½ oz) grated Parmesan cheese

1 Prick the aubergines all over with a fork and rub with a little of the oil. Place on a piece of absorbent kitchen paper and cook on HIGH for 3–4 minutes or until slightly softened. Do not overcook or the aubergines will be difficult to slice. Leave to cool while cooking the filling.

2 To make the filling, put the onion, garlic, half the cinnamon, the oregano, tomatoes and their juice, tomato purée and remaining oil in a medium bowl. Cook on HIGH for 7–8 minutes or until the onion is soft and the sauce slightly reduced, stirring two or three times.

3 Meanwhile, cut the fish into small pieces.

4 When the tomato sauce is cooked, add the fish and cook on HIGH for 4–5 minutes or until the fish flakes easily. Season to taste with salt and pepper.

5 Spoon half the fish and tomato sauce into a flameproof dish. Using a serrated knife, thinly slice the aubergines and arrange half on top of the sauce. Repeat the layers once, ending with a layer of aubergine.

6 To make the topping, beat the eggs and remaining cinnamon into the yogurt. Season generously with nutmeg and salt and pepper. Spoon evenly on top of the aubergines.

7 Cook on MEDIUM for 12–14 minutes or until the topping is set around the edge but still slightly liquid in the centre. Sprinkle with the Parmesan cheese and brown under a pre-heated grill.

# HAKE AND LIME KEBABS

## SERVES 4

700 g (1½ lb) hake fillets, skinned

2 limes

salt and pepper

1 Cut the hake into 2.5 cm (1 inch) cubes. Thinly slice 1½ limes. Thread the lime slices and the hake on to four wooden skewers. Arrange the kebabs in a single layer in a large shallow dish and squeeze the juice from the remaining half lime over them.

2 Cover the kebabs and cook on HIGH for 4–5 minutes or until the fish is cooked, repositioning the kebabs once during cooking. Season to taste with salt and pepper. Serve hot, accompanied by rice or cracked wheat.

## FISH BALLS IN A WALNUT SAUCE

### SERVES 4

450 g (1 lb) white fish fillets, such as haddock, cod or whiting

30 ml (2 tbsp) milk

50 g (2 oz) fresh wholemeal breadcrumbs

1 small onion, skinned and very finely chopped

30 ml (2 tbsp) chopped fresh coriander or parsley

salt and pepper

1 egg yolk, beaten

100 g (4 oz) walnut halves

2 garlic cloves, skinned and crushed

5 ml (1 level tsp) paprika

5 ml (1 level tsp) ground coriander

pinch of ground cloves

30 ml (2 tbsp) white wine vinegar

450 ml ($\frac{3}{4}$ pint) boiling fish or vegetable stock

walnut halves, coriander or parsley sprigs, to garnish

*1* Put the fish in a shallow dish with the milk. Cover and cook on HIGH for 4–5 minutes or until the fish flakes easily. Flake the fish, discarding the skin and any bones. Reserve the cooking liquid.

*2* Put the fish, breadcrumbs, onion, fresh coriander or parsley and salt and pepper to taste into a blender or food processor and purée until smooth. Gradually add the egg yolk to bind the mixture together to make a fairly stiff consistency.

*3* Shape the mixture into 20 walnut-sized balls. Chill in the refrigerator while making the sauce.

*4* Put the walnuts, garlic, paprika, ground coriander, cloves and vinegar into the rinsed-out bowl of the blender or food processor and purée until smooth. Transfer to a large bowl and cook on HIGH for 2 minutes, stirring frequently.

*5* Add the reserved cooking liquid and the stock to the walnut mixture and cook on HIGH for 5–6 minutes or until boiling, stirring once. Carefully add the fish balls and cook on MEDIUM for 5–6 minutes or until they feel firm to the touch, rearranging them carefully once during cooking. Garnish with walnut halves, coriander or parsley sprigs and serve hot with rice, if liked.

## KEDGEREE

### SERVES 4

225 g (8 oz) long grain white rice

salt and pepper

450 g (1 lb) smoked haddock fillets

45 ml (3 tbsp) milk

2 eggs, hard-boiled and chopped

50 g (2 oz) butter or margarine

2.5 ml ($\frac{1}{2}$ level tsp) mild curry powder (optional)

45 ml (3 tbsp) single cream

45 ml (3 tbsp) chopped fresh parsley

*1* Put the rice in a large bowl and pour over enough boiling water to cover by about 2.5 cm (1 inch). Add salt to taste, cover and cook on HIGH for 12–15 minutes or until tender. Drain and transfer to a serving dish.

*2* Put the haddock in a single layer in a large shallow dish, add the milk, cover and cook on HIGH for 4–5 minutes or until the fish flakes easily. Flake the fish, discarding the skin. Add the fish to the rice with the cooking liquid and the remaining ingredients. Season to taste with pepper.

*3* Cook on HIGH for 3–4 minutes or until hot, stirring occasionally. Serve at once.

*Fish Balls in a Walnut Sauce*

## POTATO-TOPPED FISH PIE

### SERVES 4

4 medium potatoes, each weighing about 175 g (6 oz)

50 g (2 oz) butter or margarine

450 ml (¾ pint) milk

salt and pepper

450 g (1 lb) white fish fillets, such as cod, haddock or coley

225 g (8 oz) smoked haddock

25 g (1 oz) plain flour

freshly grated nutmeg

2 eggs, hard-boiled and shelled

45 ml (3 tbsp) chopped fresh parsley

*1* Scrub the potatoes and prick all over with a fork. Arrange on absorbent kitchen paper in a circle in the cooker and cook on HIGH for 12–14 minutes or until tender, turning once. Set aside to cool slightly.

*2* Peel the potatoes and put in a bowl. Add 25 g (1 oz) butter and about 75 ml (5 tbsp) milk or enough to make a soft mashed potato. Mash thoroughly together and season to taste with salt and pepper.

*3* Put the fish in a single layer in a large shallow dish with 30 ml (2 tbsp) milk. Cover and cook on HIGH for 4–5 minutes or until the fish flakes easily.

*4* Strain the cooking liquid from the fish into a medium bowl and reserve. Remove and discard the skin and any bones from the fish. Flake the fish and put in a flameproof serving dish.

*5* Put the remaining milk and butter and the flour in the bowl with the reserved cooking liquid and cook on HIGH for 4–5 minutes or until thickened, whisking every minute. Season to taste with salt, pepper and nutmeg. Roughly chop the hard-boiled eggs

and stir into the sauce with the parsley. Pour over the fish.

*6* Spoon or pipe the mashed potato on top of the fish mixture. Cook on HIGH for 4–5 minutes or until the pie is hot, then brown under a hot grill, if liked. Serve at once with a green vegetable.

## MARBLED FISH RING

### SERVES 6

200 g (7 oz) can tuna

15 ml (1 tbsp) tomato purée

15 ml (1 tbsp) lemon juice

2 egg whites

450 ml (¾ pint) natural yogurt

salt and pepper

700 g (1½ lb) white fish fillet, such as haddock, cod or whiting, skinned

100 g (4 oz) cream cheese

30 ml (2 tbsp) chopped fresh tarragon or 10 ml (2 level tsp) dried

15 ml (1 tbsp) chopped fresh dill or 5 ml (1 level tsp) dried

fresh dill, to garnish

*1* Drain the tuna and put in a blender or food processor with the tomato purée, lemon juice, one egg white and 150 ml (¼ pint) yogurt. Purée until smooth. Season to taste with salt and pepper. Turn into a bowl and set aside.

*2* Roughly chop the white fish fillet and put in the blender or food processor with half the remaining yogurt, the egg white, cream cheese, half the tarragon and half the dill. Purée until smooth, then season with pepper to taste.

*3* Place alternate spoonfuls of the fish mixtures into a 1.1 litre (2 pint) ring mould, then draw a knife through the two mixtures in a spiral to give a marbled effect. Level the surface.

4 Cover loosely with absorbent kitchen paper, then cook on HIGH for 4–5 minutes or until the surface feels firm to the touch. Leave to cool, then chill in the refrigerator before serving.

5 When ready to serve, mix together the remaining yogurt, tarragon and dill. Season to taste with salt and pepper.

6 Turn the ring out of the mould and wipe with absorbent kitchen paper to remove any liquid. Cut into thick slices, garnish with dill and serve with the sauce.

# PAELLA

### SERVES 6–8

60 ml (4 tbsp) olive oil

1 medium onion, skinned and chopped

3 garlic cloves, skinned and crushed

450 g (1 lb) risotto rice

pinch of saffron strands

1.1 litres (2 pints) boiling fish or vegetable stock

1 red or green pepper, seeded and chopped

350 g (12 oz) tomatoes, roughly chopped

100 g (4 oz) chorizo sausage, thickly sliced

450 g (1 lb) fish fillets, such as monkfish, whiting or red bream, skinned

450 g (1 lb) fresh mussels, cleaned

6 cooked langoustines or 225 g (8 oz) cooked peeled prawns

paprika

salt and pepper

chopped fresh parsley, to garnish

1 Put the oil, onion and garlic in a large bowl. Cover and cook on HIGH for 2–3 minutes or until the onion is slightly softened.

2 Add the rice and the saffron and stir until all the rice is coated in the oil. Pour in the stock, re-cover and cook on HIGH for 12 minutes, stirring once.

3 Add the pepper, tomatoes and chorizo. Re-cover and continue to cook on HIGH for 3–5 minutes or until the rice is tender and most of the liquid is absorbed.

4 Cut the fish into small chunks and lay on top of the rice. Lay the mussels and the langoustines or prawns on top of the fish. If the rice is very dry sprinkle the fish with 30 ml (2 tbsp) water to create steam during cooking.

5 Cover and cook on HIGH for 4–5 minutes or until the fish looks opaque and the mussels have opened. Discard any unopened mussels.

6 Season generously with paprika and salt and pepper, then mix carefully together. Transfer to a large serving platter or shallow dish. Sprinkle generously with parsley and serve immediately.

# MIXED SEAFOOD WITH SAFFRON SAUCE

### SERVES 4

large pinch of saffron strands

50 ml (2 fl oz) dry white wine

strip of orange rind

1 bay leaf

450 g (1 lb) cod fillet, skinned

4 plaice quarter-cut fillets, each weighing about 50 g (2 oz), skinned

4 cooked unpeeled jumbo prawns (optional)

15 ml (1 tbsp) Greek strained yogurt

salt and pepper

fresh herbs, to garnish

*1* Put the saffron, wine, orange rind and bay leaf in a small bowl. Cook on H I G H for 2–3 minutes or until boiling. Set aside to infuse while cooking the fish.

*2* Cut the cod fillet into large chunks, and cut each plaice fillet in half. Arrange the fish and prawns, if using, in a single layer in a large shallow dish, placing the thinner pieces and the prawns towards the centre.

*3* Pour over 30 ml (2 tbsp) of the infused sauce. Cover and cook on H I G H for 5–6 minutes or until the fish is tender. Transfer the fish to four warmed serving plates.

*4* Strain the remaining wine mixture into the cooking juices remaining in the dish and stir in the yogurt. Season to taste with salt and pepper. Cook on H I G H for 1–2 minutes or until hot. Pour over the fish, garnish with herbs and serve immediately.

*Mixed Seafood with Saffron Sauce*

# TROUT WITH SESAME CREAM

### SERVES 2–4

2 trout, total weight about 275 g (10 oz)

15 ml (1 tbsp) vegetable oil

60 ml (4 tbsp) tahini (sesame seed paste)

30 ml (2 tbsp) lemon juice

150 ml ($\frac{1}{4}$ pint) soured cream

1 garlic clove, skinned and crushed (optional)

30 ml (2 tbsp) finely chopped fresh parsley

salt and pepper

tarragon or flat leaf parsley and black olives, to garnish

*1* Brush the trout with the oil and arrange in a single layer in a shallow dish. Cover and cook on H I G H for 5–7 minutes or until tender. Carefully peel off the skin, leaving the head and tail intact. Leave to cool.

*2* To make the sauce, put the tahini, lemon juice, soured cream, garlic, if using, and parsley in a bowl and mix together. Season to taste with salt and pepper.

*3* Carefully transfer the fish to two plates. Coat in some of the sauce, leaving the head and tail exposed. Garnish with tarragon or parsley leaves and olives. Serve with the remaining sauce and a salad or rice.

# SEAFOOD GUMBO

### SERVES 6

1 large onion, skinned and chopped

1–2 garlic cloves, skinned and crushed

25 g (1 oz) butter or margarine

15 ml (1 level tbsp) plain flour

900 ml (1½ pints) boiling fish or vegetable stock

4 large tomatoes, skinned and chopped

1 green pepper, seeded and chopped

225 g (8 oz) okra, trimmed and sliced

15 ml (1 tbsp) tomato purée

grated rind of 1 lemon

225 g (8 oz) cooked peeled prawns

225 g (8 oz) cooked crab meat

6 large shelled scallops

Tabasco sauce

salt and pepper

boiled rice, to serve

*1* Put the onion, garlic and butter in a large bowl. Cover and cook on HIGH for 3–4 minutes or until slightly softened.

*2* Sprinkle in the flour and cook on HIGH for 1 minute, then gradually add the stock, stirring all the time. Add the tomatoes, pepper, okra, tomato purée and lemon rind, re-cover and cook on HIGH for 6–7 minutes or until the okra is tender, stirring occasionally.

*3* Add the remaining ingredients and season to taste with Tabasco sauce and salt and pepper. Re-cover and cook on HIGH for 4–5 minutes or until the scallops are cooked and the prawns and crab meat are heated through, stirring occasionally.

*4* To serve, spoon some boiled rice into six large soup bowls and ladle the gumbo on top. Serve immediately.

# SAG PRAWNS

### SERVES 4

900 g (2 lb) fresh spinach or 450 g (1 lb) frozen leaf spinach

45 ml (3 tbsp) vegetable oil

1 small onion, skinned and finely chopped

1 garlic clove, skinned and crushed

10 ml (2 level tsp) ground ginger

10 ml (2 level tsp) garam masala

5 ml (1 level tsp) mustard seeds

2.5 ml (½ level tsp) chilli powder

2.5 ml (½ level tsp) ground turmeric

450 g (1 lb) cooked peeled prawns

60 ml (4 tbsp) desiccated coconut

salt and pepper

*1* Remove any tough stems from the fresh spinach, chop roughly and put into a bowl. Cover and cook on HIGH for 8–10 minutes or until tender, stirring once. If using frozen spinach, put into a bowl, cover and cook on HIGH for 10–12 minutes or until thawed, stirring frequently. Drain thoroughly.

*2* Put the oil, onion, garlic, ginger, garam masala, mustard seeds, chilli powder and turmeric in a bowl. Cover and cook on HIGH for 4–5 minutes or until the onion is softened.

*3* Add the prawns and stir to coat in the spicy oil. Add half the coconut and the spinach and season to taste with salt and pepper. Cover and cook on HIGH for 4–5 minutes, stirring occasionally. Serve immediately, sprinkled with the remaining coconut.

## MUSSELS IN WHITE WINE

### SERVES 2

900 g (2 lb) fresh mussels

1 small onion, skinned and finely chopped

1 garlic clove, skinned and crushed

75 ml (5 tbsp) dry white wine

75 ml (5 tbsp) fish stock or water

30 ml (2 tbsp) chopped fresh parsley

salt and pepper

*1* To clean the mussels, scrub thoroughly with a hard brush. Wash them in several changes of water.

*2* Using a sharp knife, scrape off any 'beards' or tufts protruding from the shells. Discard any damaged mussels or any open ones that do not close when tapped sharply with a knife.

*3* Put the onion, garlic, wine, stock and mussels in a large bowl. Cover and cook on HIGH for 3–5 minutes or until all the mussels have opened, removing the mussels on the top as they open and shaking the bowl occasionally. Discard any mussels that have not opened.

*4* Drain the mussels and pile into a warmed serving dish. Stir the parsley into the liquid remaining in the bowl and season with salt and pepper to taste. Pour over the mussels and serve immediately with lots of crusty bread.

## CEYLON PRAWN CURRY

### SERVES 4

50 g (2 oz) butter or margarine

1 large onion, skinned and finely chopped

1 garlic clove, skinned and crushed

15 ml (1 level tbsp) plain flour

10 ml (2 level tsp) ground turmeric

2.5 ml (½ level tsp) ground cloves

5 ml (1 level tsp) ground cinnamon

5 ml (1 level tsp) salt

5 ml (1 level tsp) sugar

50 g (2 oz) creamed coconut

450 ml (¾ pint) boiling chicken stock

450 g (1 lb) cooked peeled prawns or 12 cooked peeled Dublin Bay prawns

5 ml (1 tsp) lemon juice

fresh coriander sprigs, to garnish

boiled rice and chutney, to serve.

*1* Put the butter in a shallow dish and cook on HIGH for 1 minute or until melted. Stir in the onion and garlic, cover and cook on HIGH for 5–7 minutes or until the onion softens.

*2* Stir the flour, spices, salt and sugar into the dish and cook on HIGH for 2 minutes. Stir in the creamed coconut and stock. Cook on HIGH for 6–8 minutes or until boiling, stirring frequently.

*3* Add the prawns and lemon juice to the sauce and adjust the seasoning. Cook on HIGH for 1–2 minutes or until the prawns are heated through. Garnish with coriander and serve with rice and chutney.

# EGG NOODLES WITH SQUID, SHRIMPS AND ALMONDS

### SERVES 4–6

250 g (9 oz) packet thin egg noodles

45 ml (3 tbsp) hoisin sauce

15 ml (1 tbsp) lemon juice

30 ml (2 tbsp) soy sauce

15 ml (1 tbsp) sweet chilli sauce

45 ml (3 tbsp) sesame oil

30 ml (2 tbsp) vegetable oil

1 garlic clove, skinned and crushed

450 g (1 lb) squid, cleaned

50 g (2 oz) blanched almonds

100 g (4 oz) cooked peeled shrimps or prawns

100 g (4 oz) beansprouts

3 spring onions, trimmed and roughly chopped

black pepper

shredded lettuce and lemon wedges, to garnish

*1* Put the noodles in a large bowl and pour over about 1.7 litres (3 pints) boiling water or enough to cover the noodles by about 2.5 cm (1 inch). Cover and cook on H I G H for 2 minutes. Leave to stand while cooking the fish.

*2* Put the hoisin sauce, lemon juice, soy sauce, chilli sauce, oils and garlic in a large bowl. Cut the squid into small pieces or rings and mix into the sauce with the almonds. Cook on H I G H for 5 minutes or until the squid just looks opaque, stirring once.

*3* Add the shrimps or prawns, beansprouts and drained noodles and mix thoroughly together. Cover and cook on H I G H for 2–3 minutes or until hot, stirring once. Stir the

spring onions into the noodle mixture. Season to taste with black pepper.

*4* To serve, spoon on to plates and top each portion with a pile of shredded lettuce and a lemon wedge. Serve immediately.

# BUCKWHEAT SPAGHETTI WITH SMOKED SALMON

### SERVES 3

225 g (8 oz) buckwheat spaghetti

75 g (3 oz) smoked salmon trimmings

finely grated rind and juice of ½ small lemon

75 ml (3 fl oz) buttermilk

30 ml (2 tbsp) snipped fresh chives

1 egg, beaten

pepper

fresh chives, to garnish

*1* Break the spaghetti in half and put into a large bowl. Pour over 1.1 litres (2 pints) boiling water and stir. Cover and cook on H I G H for 5–6 minutes or until almost tender. Leave to stand, covered, while making the sauce. Do not drain.

*2* Cut the salmon into neat pieces and put in a serving bowl with the remaining ingredients and pepper to taste. Cook on H I G H for 1 minute or until slightly warmed, stirring once.

*3* Drain the pasta and rinse with boiling water. Quickly stir into the sauce and toss together to mix. Garnish with chives and serve immediately with a mixed salad.

*Egg Noodles with Squid, Shrimps and Almonds*

## SCALLOPS WITH VEGETABLES

### SERVES 4

4 spring onions, trimmed

4 medium carrots, peeled

3 medium courgettes, trimmed

12 large shelled scallops

15 ml (1 tbsp) vegetable oil

1 garlic clove, skinned and finely chopped

1.25 ml ($\frac{1}{4}$ tsp) grated fresh root ginger

1.25 ml ($\frac{1}{4}$ level tsp) five-spice powder

100 g (4 oz) beansprouts

grated rind of $\frac{1}{2}$ lemon

15 ml (1 tbsp) lemon juice

pepper

*1* Cut the spring onions into 5 cm (2 inch) lengths. Cut the carrots and courgettes into matchsticks 5 cm (2 inches) long and 0.5 cm ($\frac{1}{4}$ inch) wide.

*2* Cut the corals from the scallops and set aside. Remove the tough muscle which is found opposite the coral. Slice the scallops across the two discs.

*3* Put the oil in a large bowl and cook on HIGH for 1–2 minutes or until hot. Stir in the garlic, ginger and five-spice powder and cook on HIGH for 1 minute. Stir in the scallops and cook on HIGH for 3–4 minutes or until the scallops are opaque and tender, stirring once or twice during cooking. Remove from the bowl with a slotted spoon and set aside.

*4* Add the spring onions, carrots, courgettes and beansprouts to the bowl. Cook on HIGH for 6–7 minutes or until the vegetables are tender, stirring every minute.

*5* Return the scallops to the bowl, sprinkle over the lemon rind and juice and season to taste with pepper. Stir together, then heat on HIGH for 2 minutes. Serve hot.

## MACARONI AND SARDINE AU GRATIN

### SERVES 4–6

1 small fennel bulb, trimmed and chopped

1 medium onion, skinned and chopped

397 g (14 oz) can tomatoes

10 ml (2 tsp) tomato purée

60 ml (4 tbsp) dry white wine, or fish or vegetable stock

450 g (1 lb) sardines, cleaned and scaled

100 g (4 oz) sultanas

75 g (3 oz) pine nuts

275 g (10 oz) short cut macaroni

salt and pepper

30 ml (2 tbsp) freshly grated Parmesan cheese

50 g (2 oz) fresh breadcrumbs

*1* Put the fennel and the onion into a large gratin dish with the tomatoes, tomato purée and wine or stock. Cover and cook on HIGH for 10–12 minutes.

*2* Meanwhile, remove the heads and backbones from the sardines. Cut the sardines in half and stir into the tomato sauce with half the sultanas and pine nuts. Re-cover and cook on HIGH for 2–3 minutes.

*3* Put the macaroni into a large bowl and pour over enough boiling water to cover the pasta by about 2.5 cm (1 inch). Cover and cook on HIGH for 7–10 minutes until tender.

*4* Drain the macaroni and mix into the tomato sauce. Season to taste and lightly toss together. Level the surface.

*5* Mix the cheese and the breadcrumbs together and sprinkle on top of the pasta. Brown under a hot grill, then sprinkle with the remaining pine nuts and sultanas. Serve hot.

# MAIN DISHES

## PORK AND APRICOT GOULASH WITH CARAWAY DUMPLINGS

### SERVES 4

450 g (1 lb) pork fillet (tenderloin)

15 ml (1 tbsp) vegetable oil

1 medium onion, skinned and thinly sliced

1 green pepper, seeded and thinly sliced

15 ml (1 level tbsp) plain flour

30 ml (2 level tbsp) paprika

100 g (4 oz) no-soak dried apricots, halved

450 ml ($\frac{3}{4}$ pint) boiling chicken stock

30 ml (2 level tbsp) tomato purée

salt and pepper

100 g (4 oz) self raising flour

50 g (2 oz) shredded suet

1.25 ml ($\frac{1}{4}$ level tsp) caraway seeds

150 ml ($\frac{1}{4}$ pint) soured cream or natural yogurt

*1* Cut the pork into 0.5 cm ($\frac{1}{4}$ inch) thick pieces.

*2* Put the oil, onion and pepper in a large bowl. Cover and cook on HIGH for 5 minutes or until softened, stirring once.

*3* Stir in the plain flour and the paprika and cook, uncovered, on HIGH for 1 minute.

*4* Stir in the pork, apricots, stock, tomato purée and salt and pepper to taste. Cover and cook on HIGH for 10 minutes, stirring occasionally.

*5* Meanwhile, make the dumplings. Mix together the self raising flour, suet and caraway seeds and season to taste with salt and pepper. Add enough cold water to bind the mixture together. Roll the dough into eight small balls.

*6* Add the dumplings to the goulash, arranging them around the edge of the bowl. Re-cover and cook on HIGH for a further 5 minutes or until the pork is tender and the dumplings risen.

*7* Serve with the soured cream or yogurt spooned over.

## PORK FILLET WITH CIDER AND CORIANDER

### SERVES 4

450 g (1 lb) pork fillet (tenderloin)

15 ml (1 tbsp) vegetable oil

1 small green pepper, seeded and cut into rings

1 medium onion, skinned and chopped

15 ml (1 level tbsp) plain flour

15 ml (1 level tbsp) ground coriander

150 ml ($\frac{1}{4}$ pint) dry cider

150 ml ($\frac{1}{4}$ pint) chicken stock

salt and pepper

1 Trim the pork of all fat and membrane. Cut it into 0.5 cm ($\frac{1}{4}$ inch) thick pieces, place between two sheets of greaseproof paper and flatten with a mallet until thin.

2 Put the oil in a shallow dish and cook on HIGH for about 1 minute. Stir in the pepper and onion, cover and cook on HIGH for 5–7 minutes or until the vegetables soften.

3 Stir in the flour and coriander and cook on HIGH for 2 minutes. Gradually stir in the cider and stock and cook on HIGH for a further 3–4 minutes, stirring frequently until boiling and thickened. Add the pork, cover and cook on HIGH for 5–6 minutes or until boiling. Season to taste with salt and pepper. Stir, then continue cooking on LOW for 7–8 minutes or until the pork is tender. Leave to stand for 5 minutes before serving.

## PORK CHOPS WITH PEPPERS

### SERVES 4

1 large onion, skinned and sliced

1 large red pepper, seeded and sliced

15 ml (1 tbsp) vegetable oil

4 boneless pork chops

30 ml (2 level tbsp) paprika

150 ml ($\frac{1}{4}$ pint) double cream

salt and pepper

1 Mix the onion, red pepper and oil in a shallow dish. Cover and cook on HIGH for 5–7 minutes or until soft, stirring once.

2 Arrange the pork chops in a single layer on top of the vegetables. Blend the paprika and cream together. Season to taste with salt and pepper and pour it over the meat.

3 Cover and microwave on HIGH for 20 minutes or until the pork is tender. Serve with a green salad.

# RED CABBAGE WITH SMOKED SAUSAGE

### SERVES 4

1 medium onion, skinned and thinly sliced

30 ml (2 tbsp) vegetable oil

700 g (1½ lb) red cabbage, finely shredded

2 eating apples

450 g (1 lb) smoked sausage, such as cabanos

30 ml (2 tbsp) apple juice

15 ml (1 tbsp) horseradish sauce

2.5 ml (½ level tsp) ground allspice

salt and pepper

1 Put the onion, oil and cabbage in a large bowl and cook on HIGH for 5–8 minutes or until softened but still crisp, stirring frequently.

2 Meanwhile, core and slice the apples. Cut the sausage into chunky slices.

3 Blend the apple juice, horseradish and allspice together. Mix into the vegetables with the sausage and apple, then cook on HIGH for 3–4 minutes or until hot, stirring occasionally. Season to taste with salt and pepper. Serve hot.

# SPICED BEEF CASSEROLE

### SERVES 4

15 ml (1 tbsp) vegetable oil

1 medium onion, skinned and sliced

3 celery sticks, trimmed and chopped

1 garlic clove, skinned and crushed

50 g (2 oz) lean streaky bacon, rinded and diced

15 ml (1 level tbsp) plain flour

15 ml (1 level tbsp) mild curry powder

2.5 ml (½ level tsp) ground allspice

450 g (1 lb) lean minced beef

5 ml (1 level tsp) tomato purée

225 g (8 oz) can tomatoes

½ cucumber, chopped

25 g (1 oz) cashew nuts (optional)

150 ml (¼ pint) natural yogurt

salt and pepper

boiled rice or garlic bread, to serve

1 Put the oil in a large bowl with the onion, celery, garlic and bacon. Cover and cook on HIGH for 5–7 minutes or until the onion and celery are soft. Stir in the flour, curry powder and allspice, re-cover and cook on HIGH for 2 minutes, stirring occasionally.

2 Stir in the minced beef, tomato purée, tomatoes, cucumber and nuts, if using. Re-cover and cook on HIGH for 20–25 minutes, stirring frequently.

3 Gradually stir in the yogurt, re-cover and cook on HIGH for 2 minutes. Leave to stand for 5 minutes. Season to taste with salt and pepper.

4 Serve with rice or garlic bread.

## STEAK AND KIDNEY PUDDING

### SERVES 2

100 g (4 oz) wholemeal self raising flour

large pinch of ground mace

15 ml (1 tbsp) chopped fresh parsley

50 g (2 oz) shredded suet

salt and pepper

1 egg, beaten

15 ml (1 tbsp) vegetable oil

1 medium onion, skinned and chopped

225 g (8 oz) rump steak, cut into thin strips

1–2 lamb's kidneys, skinned, halved, cored and chopped

30 ml (2 level tbsp) plain flour

150 ml ($\frac{1}{4}$ pint) red wine

1 bay leaf

*1* To make the pastry, put the flour, mace, parsley, suet, salt and pepper into a bowl and mix together. Make a well in the centre and stir in the egg and 30–45 ml (2–3 tbsp) cold water to make a soft, light elastic dough. Knead until smooth.

*2* Roll out two thirds of the pastry on a floured surface and use to line a 600 ml (1 pint) pudding basin.

*3* Put the oil and onion in a medium bowl, cover and cook on HIGH for 5–7 minutes.

*4* Toss the steak and chopped kidneys in the flour and stir into the softened onion. Cook on HIGH for 3 minutes, then stir in the wine and bay leaf and salt and pepper to taste. Re-cover and cook on HIGH for 5 minutes or until the meat is tender, stirring occasionally.

*5* Spoon the mixture into the lined pudding basin. Roll out the remaining pastry to a circle to fit the top of the pudding. Dampen the edges and press firmly together to seal.

*6* Cover with a plate and cook on HIGH for 5 minutes, or until the pastry looks 'set'.

*7* Leave to stand for 5 minutes, then turn out on to a warmed serving dish or serve from the bowl.

## MARINATED BEEF WITH MANGE-TOUT AND WALNUTS

### SERVES 2

175 g (6 oz) lean sirloin steak

30 ml (2 tbsp) dry sherry

30 ml (2 tbsp) soy sauce

1 garlic clove, skinned and crushed

1 cm ($\frac{1}{2}$ inch) piece of fresh root ginger, peeled and grated

100 g (4 oz) mange-tout, topped and tailed

25 g (1 oz) walnuts, roughly chopped

pepper

*1* Trim the meat of all excess fat, then cut across the grain into very thin strips about 5 cm (2 inches) long. Put in a medium bowl with the sherry, soy sauce, garlic and ginger. Cover and leave to marinate for at least 1 hour.

*2* Cook on HIGH for 3 minutes, stirring once.

*3* Add the remaining ingredients and cook on HIGH for 3–4 minutes or until the beef is tender and the mange-tout just cooked, stirring occasionally. Serve hot.

## BEEF WITH GINGER AND GARLIC

### SERVES 2

350 g (12 oz) fillet steak

2.5 cm (1 inch) piece of fresh root ginger, peeled and finely grated

1 garlic clove, skinned and crushed

150 ml ($\frac{1}{4}$ pint) dry sherry

30 ml (2 tbsp) soy sauce

2 medium carrots, peeled

15 ml (1 tbsp) vegetable oil

30 ml (2 level tbsp) cornflour

2.5 ml ($\frac{1}{2}$ level tsp) light soft brown sugar

1 Cut the steak across the grain into 1 cm ($\frac{1}{2}$ inch) strips, and put into a bowl. Mix the ginger with the garlic, sherry and soy sauce. Pour over the steak, making sure that all the meat is coated, cover and leave to marinate for at least 30 minutes.

2 Using a potato peeler, cut the carrots lengthways into thin slices.

3 Put the oil in a large bowl and heat on HIGH for 1 minute or until hot. Using a slotted spoon, remove the steak from the marinade and stir into the hot oil. Cook on HIGH for 1–2 minutes or until the steak is just cooked, stirring once.

4 Meanwhile, blend the cornflour and the sugar with a little of the marinade to make a smooth paste, then gradually blend in all of the marinade.

5 Stir the carrots into the steak and cook on HIGH for 1–2 minutes, then gradually stir in the cornflour and marinade mixture. Cook on HIGH for 2–3 minutes or until boiling and thickened, stirring frequently. Serve hot.

## BEEF COOKED IN RED WINE

### SERVES 2

350 g (12 oz) chuck steak

150 ml ($\frac{1}{4}$ pint) dry red wine

1 medium onion, skinned and sliced

1 garlic clove, skinned and crushed

10 ml (2 tsp) chopped fresh oregano or 2.5 ml ($\frac{1}{2}$ level tsp) dried

salt and pepper

15 ml (1 tbsp) vegetable oil

3 streaky bacon rashers, rinded and chopped

15 ml (1 level tbsp) plain flour

chopped fresh oregano or parsley, to garnish

1 Remove any excess fat from the meat and cut into strips 5 cm (2 inches) long and 1 cm ($\frac{1}{2}$ inch) wide. Put in a shallow dish and add the wine, onion, garlic, oregano, salt and pepper. Cover and leave in the refrigerator to marinate overnight.

2 The next day, heat a large browning dish on HIGH for 5–8 minutes or according to manufacturer's instructions. Add the oil, then quickly add the bacon and cook on HIGH for 30 seconds, stirring once.

3 Remove the meat and onion from the marinade with a slotted spoon and stir into the browning dish. Cook on HIGH for 2 minutes, stirring once. Stir in the flour and cook on HIGH for 1 minute.

4 Gradually stir the marinade and 100 ml (4 fl oz) water into the dish and cook on HIGH for 4–5 minutes or until the liquid is boiling. Cover and cook on MEDIUM for 25–30 minutes, or until tender, stirring occasionally.

5 Leave to stand for 5 minutes. Adjust the seasoning if necessary, then turn into a warmed serving dish, garnish with oregano or parsley and serve.

# CHILLI CON CARNE

### SERVES 6

1 large onion, skinned and chopped

1 green pepper, seeded and cut into strips

15 ml (1 tbsp) vegetable oil

700 g (1½ lb) lean minced beef

397 g (14 oz) can chopped tomatoes

30 ml (2 tbsp) tomato purée

15 ml (1 tbsp) red wine vinegar

5 ml (1 level tsp) dark soft brown sugar

5–10 ml (1–2 level tsp) chilli powder

15 ml (1 level tbsp) ground cumin

salt and pepper

439 g (15½ oz) can red kidney beans, drained and rinsed

boiled rice and a green salad, to serve

*1* Put the onion, pepper and oil in a large bowl and mix together. Cook on HIGH for 5 minutes or until softened, stirring once. Add the beef, breaking up any large pieces. Cook on HIGH for 6–8 minutes or until the meat starts to change colour, stirring after 3 minutes.

*2* Mix together the tomatoes, tomato purée, vinegar, sugar, chilli powder and cumin. Season to taste with salt and pepper, then stir into the meat. Cover and cook on HIGH for 30 minutes, stirring once halfway through.

*3* Stir in the beans, re-cover the dish and continue cooking on HIGH for 5 minutes. Serve with boiled rice and a green salad.

*Lamb with Aubergine and Mint*

# LAMB WITH AUBERGINE AND MINT

### SERVES 4

1 large aubergine, weighing about 400 g (14 oz)

salt and pepper

450 g (1 lb) lean boneless lamb, such as fillet or leg

30 ml (2 tbsp) olive oil

397 g (14 oz) can tomatoes, drained

a few allspice berries, crushed

small bunch of fresh mint

*1* Cut the aubergine into 2.5 cm (1 inch) cubes. Put in a colander, sprinkling each layer generously with salt. Stand the colander on a large plate, cover with a small plate and place a weight on top. Leave for about 20 minutes to extract the bitter juices.

*2* Meanwhile, trim the meat of all excess fat and cut into 2.5 cm (1 inch) cubes. Rinse the aubergine and pat dry.

*3* Heat a large browning dish on HIGH for 5–8 minutes or according to manufacturer's instructions.

*4* Put the oil in the browning dish, then quickly add the meat. Cook on HIGH for 2 minutes.

*5* Turn the pieces of meat over and cook on HIGH for a further 2 minutes.

*6* Add the aubergine to the browning dish and cook on HIGH for 5 minutes, stirring once.

*7* Add the tomatoes, breaking them up with a fork, the allspice and pepper to taste. Cover and cook on HIGH for about 15 minutes or until the lamb and aubergine are very tender, stirring occasionally.

*8* Coarsely chop the mint and stir into the lamb with salt to taste. Re-cover and cook on HIGH for 1 minute. Serve hot with cooked brown rice.

## LAMB AND APRICOT KEBABS

### SERVES 4

700 g (1½ lb) lamb fillet or boned leg of lamb

60 ml (4 tbsp) olive oil

juice of 1 lemon

1 garlic clove, skinned and crushed

pinch of salt

5 ml (1 level tsp) ground cumin

5 ml (1 level tsp) ground coriander

5 ml (1 level tsp) ground cinnamon

2 large onions, skinned and quartered

75 g (3 oz) no-soak dried apricots, diced

8 bay leaves

cooked rice, to serve

*1* Cut the lamb into 2.5 cm (1 inch) thick slices if using fillet, or cubes if using leg.

*2* Put the olive oil, lemon juice, garlic, salt, cumin, coriander and cinnamon in a large bowl and whisk together well. Stir in the lamb, cover and leave to marinate at room temperature for at least 4 hours.

*3* Put the onion quarters and apricots in a medium bowl, add 150 ml (¼ pint) water, cover and cook on HIGH for 3 minutes. Drain well, then re-cover and set aside until the lamb is ready for cooking.

*4* Thread alternate pieces of lamb, apricot, onion quarters and bay leaves on to eight wooden kebab skewers.

*5* Arrange the kebabs in a double layer on a roasting rack in a shallow dish and spoon over any remaining marinade. Cook on HIGH for 8 minutes, then re-position the kebabs so that the inside skewers are moved to the outside of the dish. Cook on HIGH for 10 minutes, re-positioning the kebabs twice during this cooking period. Leave to stand for 5 minutes.

*6* Serve with rice. The juices left in the bottom of the cooking dish may be re-heated and served separately with the kebabs, if liked.

## CINNAMON LAMB WITH ALMONDS AND APRICOTS

### SERVES 2

25 g (1 oz) whole blanched almonds

50 g (2 oz) no-soak dried apricots, halved

350 g (12 oz) lamb fillet

15 ml (1 level tbsp) plain flour

10 ml (2 level tsp) ground cinnamon

2.5 ml (½ level tsp) ground cumin

salt and pepper

15 ml (1 tbsp) vegetable oil

75 ml (3 fl oz) chicken stock

1 bay leaf

30 ml (2 tbsp) natural yogurt

*1* Put the almonds on a large flat plate and cook on HIGH for 6 minutes or until lightly browned, stirring occasionally. Set aside.

*2* Put the apricots in a small bowl with 150 ml (¼ pint) water. Cover and cook on HIGH for 5 minutes. Leave to stand.

*3* Heat a large browning dish on HIGH for 5–8 minutes or according to manufacturer's instructions.

*4* Meanwhile, cut the lamb into 2.5 cm (1 inch) slices. Cover the slices with grease-proof paper and flatten them slightly with a rolling pin. Cut each slice in half.

*5* Mix the flour, cinnamon, cumin and salt and pepper to taste together and use to coat the meat.

*6* Add the oil to the browning dish, then quickly stir in the meat. Cook on HIGH for 2 minutes, then turn the meat over and cook on HIGH for 2 minutes.

7 Stir in the stock and bay leaf and mix well together. Cover and cook on L O W for 10 minutes or until the meat is tender, stirring occasionally.

8 Drain the apricots and stir into the dish. Cook on H I G H for 2–3 minutes or until the apricots are hot. Stir in the yogurt and more seasoning if necessary. Serve hot, sprinkled with the toasted almonds.

4 Heat a large browning dish on H I G H for 5–8 minutes or according to manufacturer's instructions. Add the oil, then quickly add the lamb. Cook on H I G H for 2 minutes or until lightly browned on one side. Turn the lamb over and cook on H I G H for 1–2 minutes more or until the second side is brown.

5 Pour the sauce over the lamb in the browning dish, stirring to loosen any sediment at the bottom of the dish. Cook on H I G H for 3–4 minutes or until the lamb is tender, stirring occasionally. Serve hot.

# PROVENÇAL LAMB FILLET

### SERVES 4

2 medium courgettes, trimmed

397 g (14 oz) can tomatoes

1 garlic clove, skinned and crushed

1 medium onion, skinned and finely chopped

15 ml (1 tbsp) tomato purée

60 ml (4 tbsp) dry red wine

1 bay leaf

fresh thyme sprig or pinch of dried

a few basil leaves or pinch of dried

salt and pepper

450 g (1 lb) lamb fillet

15 ml (1 tbsp) vegetable oil

1 Cut the courgettes into 1 cm (½ inch) slices. Put in a large bowl with the tomatoes and juice, garlic, onion, tomato purée, wine, herbs and salt and pepper to taste.

2 Cook on H I G H for 15 minutes or until the sauce is slightly reduced and thickened, stirring once or twice during cooking.

3 Meanwhile, cut the lamb into 1 cm (½ inch) slices. Cover the slices with greaseproof paper and flatten them with a rolling pin.

## MARINATED CHICKEN WITH PEANUT SAUCE

### SERVES 4

60 ml (4 tbsp) olive oil

30 ml (2 tbsp) herb vinegar

10 ml (2 level tsp) Dijon mustard

grated rind and juice of ½ lemon

15 ml (1 tbsp) soy sauce

1 garlic clove, skinned and crushed

salt and pepper

4 chicken breast fillets, skinned

lemon and lime slices, to garnish

*For the sauce*

1 small onion, skinned and chopped

2 large tomatoes, skinned and chopped

1 garlic clove, skinned and chopped

15 ml (1 tbsp) tomato purée

1.25–2.5 ml (¼–½ level tsp) cayenne pepper

75 ml (3 fl oz) chicken stock

15 ml (1 tbsp) soy sauce

60 ml (4 level tbsp) peanut butter

*1* To make the marinade, whisk together the oil, vinegar, mustard, lemon rind and juice, soy sauce, garlic and salt and pepper to taste until well blended.

*2* Cut the chicken into 2.5 cm (1 inch) cubes and thread on to eight wooden kebab skewers. Place in a shallow dish and pour the marinade over. Cover and leave to stand for at least 2 hours or overnight.

*3* Purée all the ingredients for the sauce in a blender or food processor. Pour the sauce into a bowl, cover and set aside.

*4* Cook the chicken, covered, on HIGH for 10–12 minutes or until cooked, turning and re-positioning at least twice during cooking.

*5* Arrange the chicken in a serving dish. Reserve the cooking liquid and keep it hot while heating the sauce.

*6* Add the reserved cooking liquid to the sauce mixture, cover and cook on HIGH for 5–6 minutes or until boiling, stirring frequently.

*7* Garnish the chicken with slices of lemon and lime. Pour the sauce into a serving jug or bowl and serve separately with the chicken.

## SESAME CHICKEN WITH PEPPERS

### SERVES 4

4 chicken breast fillets, skinned

1 large red pepper, seeded

1 large yellow pepper, seeded

6 spring onions, trimmed and sliced

2.5 cm (1 inch) piece of fresh root ginger, peeled and grated

225 g (8 oz) can sliced bamboo shoots, drained

30 ml (2 tbsp) vegetable oil

30 ml (2 level tbsp) sesame seeds

30 ml (2 tbsp) soy sauce

30 ml (2 tbsp) dry sherry

*1* Cut the chicken and peppers into thin strips and put in a large bowl with all the other ingredients. Stir well to mix.

*2* Cook on HIGH for 5–6 minutes or until the chicken is tender and the vegetables are tender but still firm, stirring occasionally. Serve hot.

*Marinated Chicken with Peanut Sauce*

# CHICKEN AND PINE NUT KOFTAS

### SERVES 4

2 small thin slices of white bread, crusts removed

4 chicken breast fillets, skinned

50 g (2 oz) pine nuts

45 ml (3 tbsp) chopped fresh parsley

small pinch of ground cinnamon

pinch of paprika

1 egg

salt and pepper

lemon wedges, to garnish

Fresh Tomato Sauce (see page 172), to serve

*1* Put the bread in a blender or food processor and process to form bread-crumbs. Add the chicken and process until finely minced.

*2* Add the pine nuts, parsley, cinnamon, paprika, egg, and salt and pepper to taste, and process again quickly until combined.

*3* With wet hands, shape the mixture into 16 equal-sized balls. Arrange in a single layer in a shallow dish. Cook on HIGH for 5–6 minutes or until the meat is cooked, rearranging once during cooking.

*4* Garnish the koftas with lemon wedges and serve with tomato sauce. Accompany with cooked rice, if liked.

*Marinated Chicken with Peppers and Marjoram*

# MARINATED CHICKEN WITH PEPPERS AND MARJORAM

### SERVES 2

2 chicken breast fillets, skinned

1 garlic clove, skinned and crushed

10 ml (2 tsp) lemon juice

pinch of sugar

45 ml (3 tbsp) olive or vegetable oil

15 ml (1 tbsp) chopped fresh marjoram or 5 ml (1 level tsp) dried

1 small onion, skinned and thinly sliced into rings

salt and pepper

1 small red pepper

1 small yellow pepper

50 g (2 oz) black olives, halved and stoned

15 ml (1 level tbsp) capers

fresh marjoram, to garnish

*1* Cut the chicken breasts in half widthways, and put in a shallow dish.

*2* Put the garlic, lemon juice and sugar in a small bowl and blend together. Gradually whisk in the oil. Stir in the marjoram and onion rings and salt and pepper to taste. Pour over the chicken, cover and leave to marinate for at least 30 minutes.

*3* Meanwhile, seed the peppers and cut into large chunks. Put into a shallow dish with 30 ml (2 tbsp) water, cover and cook on HIGH for 5–6 minutes or until the peppers are just soft, stirring occasionally. Drain and set aside.

*4* Cook the chicken, covered, on HIGH for 5–6 minutes, or until tender, turning once.

*5* Add the peppers, olives and capers and cook on HIGH for 1–2 minutes or until heated through, stirring once. Serve immediately, garnished with fresh marjoram.

## SPANISH CHICKEN

### SERVES 4

15 ml (1 tbsp) vegetable oil

15 g ($\frac{1}{2}$ oz) butter or margarine

4 chicken joints

397 g (14 oz) can tomatoes

1 Spanish onion, skinned and finely sliced

1 red pepper, seeded and sliced

1 green pepper, seeded and sliced

2.5 ml ($\frac{1}{2}$ level tsp) dried basil

salt and pepper

15 ml (1 level tbsp) cornflour

*1* Heat a large browning dish on HIGH for 5–8 minutes or according to manufacturer's instructions. Add the oil and butter, then quickly add the chicken joints, skin side down. Cook on HIGH for 3 minutes, then turn the joints over.

*2* Meanwhile, push the tomatoes, with their juice, through a sieve. Stir the tomato purée into the chicken with the onion, peppers, basil and salt and pepper to taste. Cover and continue to cook on HIGH for 12 minutes, re-positioning the chicken twice during cooking.

*3* Reduce the setting to LOW and cook for a further 10 minutes or until the chicken is tender.

*4* Remove the chicken pieces to a warmed serving dish. Blend the cornflour to a paste with a little cold water and stir this into the juices in the browning dish. Cook on HIGH for 5 minutes, stirring once. Pour over the chicken and serve.

## TURKEY STROGANOFF

### SERVES 4

50 g (2 oz) butter or margarine

1 large onion, skinned and sliced

450 g (1 lb) turkey breast fillet, skinned and cut into thin strips

225 g (8 oz) mushrooms, sliced

150 ml ($\frac{1}{4}$ pint) white wine or chicken stock

150 ml ($\frac{1}{4}$ pint) soured cream

30 ml (2 tbsp) tomato purée

15 ml (1 tbsp) wholegrain mustard

10 ml (2 level tsp) paprika

1 egg yolk

salt and pepper

*1* Put the butter in a large bowl and cook on HIGH for 45 seconds or until melted. Stir in the onion and cook on HIGH for 5–7 minutes or until the onion is soft, stirring once.

*2* Stir in the turkey, mushrooms and wine. Cook on HIGH for 7 minutes or until the turkey is tender, stirring occasionally.

*3* Mix all the remaining ingredients together, adding salt and pepper to taste. Add to the meat and cook on MEDIUM for 4–5 minutes or until thickened, stirring after each minute. Do not allow to boil. Serve with rice or pasta.

## SHREDDED TURKEY WITH COURGETTES

### SERVES 4

450 g (1 lb) turkey breast fillets

450 g (1 lb) courgettes, trimmed

1 red pepper, seeded

45 ml (3 tbsp) vegetable oil

45 ml (3 tbsp) dry sherry

15 ml (1 tbsp) soy sauce

salt and pepper

60 ml (4 tbsp) natural yogurt or soured cream

1 Cut the turkey, courgettes and pepper into fine strips to ensure even cooking.

2 Place all the ingredients, except the yogurt, in a medium bowl, adding salt and pepper to taste. Stir well to mix.

3 Cover and cook on HIGH for 4 minutes or until the turkey and vegetables are tender.

4 Leave to stand for 5 minutes, then add the yogurt, adjust the seasoning and serve.

## DUCK IN SWEET AND SOUR SAUCE

### SERVES 2

2 duck breast fillets, each weighing about 200 g (7 oz)

1 orange

30 ml (2 tbsp) soy sauce

15 ml (1 level tbsp) dark soft brown sugar

15 ml (1 tbsp) clear honey

15 ml (1 tbsp) red wine vinegar

5 ml (1 tsp) sherry

pinch of ground ginger

salt and pepper

15 ml (1 level tbsp) cornflour

1 Put the duck in a large shallow dish. Cut the orange in half and squeeze the juice from one half over the duck. Cut the other half into slices and reserve for the garnish.

2 Mix the remaining ingredients, except the cornflour, with 30 ml (2 tbsp) water and pour over the duck. Cover and leave to marinate for at least 30 minutes, turning once.

3 Remove the duck from the marinade, leaving the marinade in the dish. Prick the duck skin with a fork. Place the duck, skin side up, on a roasting rack in a large shallow dish. Cover with a split roasting bag and cook on HIGH for 5 minutes or until the skin is just starting to brown. Leave to stand.

4 Cook the reserved marinade on HIGH for 2–3 minutes or until boiling, then add the duck portions, skin side down. Re-cover and cook on LOW for 8–10 minutes until tender.

5 Transfer the duck to a serving dish and carve into thick slices. Blend the cornflour to a smooth paste with a little water and stir into the sauce. Cook on HIGH for 2 minutes or until boiling and thickened, stirring occasionally. Spoon over the duck and garnish with the reserved orange slices.

# PEKING STYLE DUCK

### SERVES 4

1 bunch of spring onions

½ cucumber

2 kg (4 lb) oven-ready duckling

soy sauce

100 ml (4 fl oz) hoisin sauce

*For the pancakes*

450 g (1 lb) plain flour

pinch of salt

15 ml (1 tbsp) vegetable oil plus extra for brushing

*1* Trim the root ends of the spring onions and trim the green leaves down to about 5 cm (2 inches). Skin, then cut twice lengthways to within 2.5 cm (1 inch) of the white end. Place in a bowl of iced water and refrigerate for 1–2 hours or until the onions curl. Cut the cucumber into 5 cm (2 inch) fingers.

*2* To make the pancakes, place the flour and salt in a large bowl. Gradually mix in 15 ml (1 tbsp) oil and 375 ml (13 fl oz) boiling water, stirring vigorously with a wooden spoon. Leave to cool slightly, then shape into a ball and turn on to a lightly floured surface. Knead for about 5 minutes to make a soft smooth dough. Leave to stand in a bowl for 30 minutes covered with a damp cloth or cling film.

*3* Cut the dough in half and shape each half into a roll 40 cm (16 inches) long. Cut each roll into 16 even slices. On a lightly floured surface, roll out 2 slices of dough into circles about 7.5 cm (3 inches) across. Brush the tops with oil. Put the oiled surfaces together and roll out to a thin 15 cm (6 inch) circle. Repeat with the remaining dough to make a total of 16 pairs of pancakes.

*4* Heat an ungreased frying pan or griddle and cook each pair of pancakes for about 1–2 minutes on each side, turning when air bubbles start to form. Remove from the frying pan and separate the pancakes while they are still hot. Stack in a clean damp tea-towel.

*5* Pat the duck dry with absorbent kitchen paper. Calculate the cooking time at 10 minutes per 450 g (1 lb). Place the duck breast side down on a roasting rack and brush with soy sauce.

*6* Cover and cook on HIGH for the calculated cooking time. Turn the duck over halfway through cooking, brush with soy sauce and continue to cook on HIGH, uncovered, until the duck is tender. Leave the duck to stand, loosely covered with foil.

*7* Grill the duck under a hot grill for about 2 minutes or until golden brown and the skin is crisp on all sides.

*8* Place the hoisin sauce in a small bowl and cook on HIGH for about 2 minutes or until just bubbling.

*9* Cut the duck into small pieces. Meanwhile, heat the pancakes wrapped in the damp tea-towel on HIGH for 2 minutes or until just warm.

*10* Serve each person with eight pancakes and some of the duck, including the skin. Hand round the vegetables and sauce separately. To eat, spread a little sauce on a pancake and top with vegetables and duck. Roll up and eat with your fingers.

*Peking Style Duck*

## LIVER AND BEAN CASSEROLE

### SERVES 4

350 g (12 oz) lamb's liver, washed

25 g (1 oz) plain flour

15 ml (1 tbsp) vegetable oil

1 medium onion, skinned and finely chopped

150 ml ($\frac{1}{4}$ pint) beef stock

75 ml (3 fl oz) milk

30 ml (2 tbsp) tomato purée

5 ml (1 level tsp) dried mixed herbs

100 g (4 oz) mushrooms, sliced

475 g (17 oz) can red kidney beans, drained

salt and pepper

*1* Cut the liver into 1 cm ($\frac{1}{2}$ inch) strips and toss in the flour.

*2* Heat a browning dish on HIGH for 5–8 minutes or according to manufacturer's instructions. Add the oil, then quickly add the liver, any excess flour and the onion. Mix well and cook on HIGH for 3 minutes, stirring occasionally.

*3* Add the stock, milk, tomato purée and herbs and mix well together. Cook on HIGH for 10 minutes or until boiling, stirring occasionally.

*4* Add the mushrooms, kidney beans and salt and pepper to taste and cook on HIGH for 5–7 minutes or until the liver is tender. Serve hot with boiled rice or mashed potatoes and a green vegetable.

## LIVER WITH ONIONS AND MUSHROOMS

### SERVES 4

450 g (1 lb) lamb's liver

15 ml (1 level tbsp) plain flour

50 g (2 oz) butter or margarine

450 g (1 lb) onions, skinned and thinly sliced

4 streaky bacon rashers, rinded and chopped

100 g (4 oz) mushrooms, sliced

salt and pepper

15 ml (1 tbsp) wine vinegar

*1* Wash the liver in cold water and cut out any inedible parts. Pat dry with absorbent kitchen paper, then cut diagonally into thick slices. Toss gently in the flour.

*2* Heat a large browning dish on HIGH for 5–8 minutes or according to manufacturer's instructions. Add 25 g (1 oz) butter and quickly add the liver. Cook on HIGH for about 5 minutes, turning the slices over and repositioning them after 3 minutes. Remove the liver to a hot dish, cover and keep warm.

*3* Add the remaining butter to the browning dish and cook on HIGH for about 1 minute or until bubbling.

*4* Stir the onions, bacon and mushrooms into the butter, cover and cook on HIGH for 5–7 minutes or until softened, stirring frequently.

*5* Season the onions very well with salt and pepper and stir in the vinegar and liver. Reheat on HIGH for 1 minute and serve hot.

## KIDNEYS AND MUSHROOMS IN SOURED CREAM SAUCE

### SERVES 4

30 ml (2 tbsp) vegetable oil

700 g (1½ lb) lambs' kidneys, skinned, halved and cored

100 g (4 oz) button mushrooms

30 ml (2 tbsp) white wine

150 ml (¼ pint) soured cream

freshly grated nutmeg

salt and pepper

cooked rice, to serve

1 Put the oil in a large shallow dish and cook on HIGH for 1 minute or until hot. Add the kidneys and mushrooms and toss together to coat in the oil. Cook on HIGH for 5–6 minutes or until cooked, stirring frequently.

2 Transfer the kidneys and mushrooms to a serving dish, then stir the wine into the juices left in the cooking dish. Cook on HIGH for 3 minutes or until boiling. Stir in the cream and cook on HIGH for 1 minute or until hot.

3 Strain the sauce over the kidneys and mushrooms and season generously with nutmeg and salt and pepper. Cook on HIGH for 1 minute or until heated through, stirring occasionally, then serve immediately, with rice to mop up the juices.

## GROUNDNUT STEW

### SERVES 4

15 ml (1 tbsp) vegetable oil

15 ml (1 level tbsp) paprika

5 ml (1 level tsp) ground cumin

2.5 ml (½ level tsp) chilli powder

100 g (4 oz) unsalted peanuts

4 chicken breast fillets, skinned

30 ml (2 tbsp) soy sauce

1 garlic clove, skinned and crushed

1 fresh green chilli, seeded and chopped (optional)

3 large tomatoes, chopped

grated rind and juice of 1 lime (optional)

cooked rice, to serve

1 Put the oil, paprika, cumin, chilli and peanuts in a shallow dish. Cook on HIGH for 5 minutes, stirring occasionally. Set aside.

2 Cut the chicken into 2.5 cm (1 inch) cubes and place in a medium bowl with the soy sauce and garlic. Cover and cook on HIGH for 5 minutes.

3 Meanwhile, put the peanut mixture, chilli, if used, tomatoes, lime rind and juice, if used, and 150 ml (¼ pint) water in a blender or food processor and purée until almost smooth.

4 Add the purée to the chicken and stir well to mix. Cook on HIGH for 5–7 minutes or until the chicken is very tender, stirring occasionally. Serve hot, with rice.

## CALF'S LIVER WITH APPLE, BACON AND SAGE

### SERVES 2

225 g (8 oz) calf's liver, washed

15 ml (1 level tbsp) plain flour

salt and pepper

paprika

15 ml (1 tbsp) vegetable oil

15 g ($\frac{1}{2}$ oz) butter or margarine

3 streaky bacon rashers, rinded

1 red eating apple

1 medium onion, skinned and thinly sliced

200 ml (7 fl oz) medium dry cider

30 ml (2 tbsp) soured cream

5 ml (1 tsp) chopped fresh sage or 2.5 ml ($\frac{1}{2}$ level tsp) dried

fresh sage, to garnish

*1* Cut the liver into thin strips, trimming away any inedible parts. Coat in the flour and season well with salt, pepper and paprika.

*2* Put the oil and butter in a shallow dish and cook on HIGH for 30 seconds or until the butter melts.

*3* Meanwhile, cut the bacon into thin strips. Core the apple, cut into rings, then cut each ring in half.

*4* Stir the onion and bacon into the fat and cook on HIGH for 5–6 minutes or until the onion is softened, stirring frequently.

*5* Stir in the liver and cook on HIGH for 1–2 minutes or until the liver just changes colour, stirring occasionally. Stir in the apple slices and 150 ml ($\frac{1}{4}$ pint) cider and cook on HIGH for 2–3 minutes or until the liver is tender, stirring occasionally. Remove the liver, bacon, apple and onion with a slotted spoon and transfer to a warmed serving dish.

*6* Stir the remaining cider into the dish with the cream and sage and cook on HIGH for 4–5 minutes or until thickened and reduced. Adjust the seasoning, if necessary.

*7* Reheat the liver and apple mixture on HIGH for 1 minute, if necessary, then pour over the sauce. Garnish with sage and serve immediately.

## RISOTTO ALLA MILANESE

### SERVES 4

75 g (3 oz) butter or margarine

1 small onion, skinned and finely chopped

450 g (1 lb) arborio rice

150 ml ($\frac{1}{4}$ pint) dry white wine

750 ml (1$\frac{1}{4}$ pints) boiling vegetable or chicken stock

2.5 ml ($\frac{1}{2}$ level tsp) saffron powder or large pinch of saffron strands

75 g (3 oz) freshly grated Parmesan cheese

salt and pepper

*1* Put half the butter and the onion in a large bowl. Cover and cook on HIGH for 3–4 minutes or until the onion is softened. Add the rice, wine, stock and saffron, re-cover and cook on HIGH for 13–15 minutes or until the rice is tender and the water absorbed.

*2* Stir in the remaining butter and half of the cheese, then season generously with pepper and a little salt. Serve immediately, with the remaining Parmesan handed round separately and accompanied by a mixed salad.

*Calf's Liver with Apple, Bacon and Sage*

## GREEK STUFFED AUBERGINES

### SERVES 4

30 ml (2 tbsp) olive oil

2 garlic cloves, skinned and crushed

5 ml (1 level tsp) ground allspice

5 ml (1 level tsp) ground cinnamon

30 ml (2 tbsp) tomato purée

5 ml (1 tsp) mint sauce

50 g (2 oz) long grain white rice

225 ml (8 fl oz) boiling vegetable stock

225 g (8 oz) minced lamb

2 medium aubergines, each weighing about 350 g (12 oz)

2 eggs, beaten

salt and pepper

*1* Put 15 ml (1 tbsp) of the oil, the garlic, allspice and cinnamon in a large bowl and cook on HIGH for 1–2 minutes or until the garlic softens.

*2* Add the tomato purée, mint sauce, rice and stock, cover and cook on HIGH for 10–12 minutes or until the rice is tender and the liquid is absorbed.

*3* Stir in the lamb and cook on HIGH for 5–10 minutes or until the meat changes colour, stirring occasionally.

*4* Halve the aubergines lengthways, and scoop out the flesh, leaving a 1 cm (½ inch) shell. Finely chop the flesh and add to the meat mixture. Cook on HIGH for 5 minutes. Stir in the egg and season to taste with salt and pepper.

*5* Brush the aubergine shells, inside and out, with the remaining oil. Spoon in the meat filling. Arrange in a serving dish and cook on HIGH for 8–10 minutes or until the filling is set and the aubergine really soft. Serve warm with a green salad.

## TOMATO AND OKRA CURRY

### SERVES 4

30 ml (2 tbsp) vegetable oil

2 medium onions, skinned and thinly sliced

2 garlic cloves, skinned and crushed

15 ml (1 level tbsp) poppy seeds

10 ml (2 level tsp) cumin seeds

10 ml (2 level tsp) fennel seeds

5 ml (1 level tsp) ground turmeric

450 g (1 lb) ripe tomatoes, roughly chopped

15 ml (1 tbsp) tomato purée

450 g (1 lb) small okra, trimmed

30 ml (2 tbsp) lemon juice

10 ml (2 level tsp) garam masala

30 ml (2 tbsp) chopped fresh coriander

salt and pepper

fresh coriander, to garnish

*1* Put the oil, onion and garlic in a large bowl, cover and cook on HIGH for 10–12 minutes or until the onions are very soft, stirring occasionally.

*2* Add the poppy seeds, cumin seeds, fennel seeds and ground turmeric and cook on HIGH for 2 minutes or until the spices release their aroma, stirring once. Add the tomatoes, tomato purée, okra, lemon juice and 150 ml (¼ pint) water. Re-cover and cook on HIGH for 10–12 minutes or until the okra is tender.

*3* Stir in the garam masala and the coriander and season to taste with salt and pepper. Serve immediately, garnished with coriander.

## PARSNIP AND BUTTERBEAN GRATIN

### SERVES 4–6

50 g (2 oz) butter or margarine

50 g (2 oz) plain wholemeal flour

750 ml (1¼ pints) milk

300 ml (½ pint) boiling vegetable stock

900 g (2 lb) parsnips, peeled

4 large carrots, peeled

450 g (1 lb) cooked butterbeans, or two 440 g (15½ oz) cans, drained and rinsed

175 g (6 oz) mature Cheddar cheese

salt and pepper

50 g (2 oz) granary or wholemeal breadcrumbs

1 Put the butter, flour, milk and stock in a large bowl and cook on HIGH for 5–7 minutes or until boiling and thickened, stirring frequently.

2 Meanwhile, cut the parsnips into 2.5 cm (1 inch) chunks and cut the carrots into 1 cm (½ inch) slices. Add the parsnips and carrots to the sauce. Cover and cook on HIGH for 20–25 minutes or until tender, stirring occasionally.

3 Add the butterbeans and 100 g (4 oz) cheese and season to taste with salt and pepper. Cook on HIGH for 2 minutes or until the cheese melts. Spoon into a gratin dish.

4 Mix the remaining cheese with the breadcrumbs and sprinkle on top of the stew. Brown under a hot grill. Serve with brown rice or a salad and brown bread.

## MEXICAN CHILLI BEANS

### SERVES 3–4

15 ml (1 tbsp) olive oil

1 onion, skinned and chopped

2 garlic cloves, skinned and crushed

1 green chilli, seeded and chopped

450 g (1 lb) cooked beans such as red kidney, pinto or black beans, or two 425 g (15 oz) cans beans, drained and rinsed

30 ml (2 tbsp) tomato purée

450 ml (¾ pint) vegetable stock

salt and pepper

*To serve*

1 ripe avocado

100 g (4 oz) Cheddar cheese, grated

30 ml (2 tbsp) chopped fresh coriander

1 Put the oil, onion, garlic and chilli in a large bowl, cover and cook on HIGH for 4–5 minutes or until slightly softened.

2 Add the beans, tomato purée and stock, re-cover and cook on HIGH for 7–8 minutes or until boiling, stirring occasionally.

3 Using a slotted spoon, remove 60 ml (4 tbsp) of the beans from the bowl and mash with a fork. Return to the bowl and mix thoroughly. Season to taste with salt and pepper, then re-cover and cook on HIGH for a further 3–4 minutes or until thickened.

4 Meanwhile, peel and stone the avocado. Cut the flesh into neat pieces.

5 To serve, spoon the beans into individual bowls, then top each serving with grated cheese and avocado. Sprinkle with the coriander. Serve hot with brown rice or granary bread.

## BEAN GOULASH

### SERVES 4–6

100 g (4 oz) black-eye beans, soaked overnight

100 g (4 oz) aduki beans, soaked overnight

15 ml (1 tbsp) vegetable oil

1 garlic clove, skinned and crushed

1 yellow pepper, seeded and roughly chopped

10 ml (2 level tsp) caraway seeds, lightly crushed

15 ml (1 level tbsp) paprika

397 g (14 oz) can chopped tomatoes

175 g (6 oz) mushrooms, thickly sliced

60 ml (4 tbsp) natural yogurt

salt and pepper

chopped fresh parsley, to garnish

*1* Drain the beans and put in a large bowl. Pour over enough boiling water to cover by about 2.5 cm (1 inch). Cover and cook on HIGH for 25–30 minutes or until tender. Leave to stand, covered. Do not drain.

*2* Meanwhile, put the oil, garlic, yellow pepper, caraway seeds and paprika in a large serving bowl. Cover and cook on HIGH for 2 minutes, stirring once.

*3* Drain the beans, rinse with boiling water and add to the pepper with the tomatoes and mushrooms. Re-cover and cook on HIGH for 8–10 minutes, stirring once. Stir in 30 ml (2 tbsp) of the yogurt and season to taste with salt and pepper. Drizzle the remaining yogurt on top and sprinkle with the parsley. Serve hot with brown rice.

## MUSHROOM, COURGETTE AND BEAN STEW

### SERVES 4

25 g (1 oz) butter or margarine

1 medium onion, skinned and chopped

25 g (1 oz) plain wholemeal flour

450 ml ($\frac{3}{4}$ pint) boiling vegetable stock

15 ml (1 level tbsp) mild wholegrain mustard

450 g (1 lb) cooked beans such as flageolet, borlotti or black-eye beans, or two 425 g (15 oz) cans beans, drained and rinsed

225 g (8 oz) mushrooms, halved if large

450 g (1 lb) courgettes, trimmed

45 ml (3 tbsp) chopped fresh mixed herbs

salt and pepper

*1* Put the butter and onion in a large bowl. Cover and cook on HIGH for 2–3 minutes or until slightly softened. Stir in the flour and cook on HIGH for 1 minute, then gradually stir in the stock.

*2* Cook on HIGH for 4–5 minutes or until boiling and thickened, stirring frequently.

*3* Add the mustard, beans and mushrooms and cook on HIGH for 2–3 minutes.

*4* Meanwhile, cut the courgettes into 1 cm ($\frac{1}{2}$ inch) slices. Stir the courgettes and half of the herbs into the stew. Cover and cook on HIGH for 5–6 minutes or until the courgettes are just cooked. Season to taste with salt and pepper and stir in the remaining herbs.

*Bean Goulash*

# BEAN MOUSSAKA

### SERVES 4

2 aubergines, each weighing about 225 g (8 oz)

15 ml (1 tbsp) vegetable oil

1 medium onion, skinned and finely chopped

1 garlic clove, skinned and crushed

large pinch of ground cinnamon

5 ml (1 level tsp) dried oregano

397 g (14 oz) can tomatoes

15 ml (1 tbsp) tomato purée

450 g (1 lb) cooked beans such as red kidney, chick-peas, flageolet, haricot beans or a mixture, or two 425 g (15 oz) cans beans, drained and rinsed

salt and pepper

2 eggs, beaten

300 ml (½ pint) natural yogurt

freshly grated nutmeg

30 ml (2 level tbsp) grated Parmesan cheese

1 Prick the aubergines all over with a fork and rub with a little of the oil. Place on absorbent kitchen paper and cook on HIGH for 4–5 minutes or until slightly softened. Do not overcook or the aubergines will be difficult to slice. Leave to cool while cooking the filling.

2 To make the filling, put the onion, garlic, cinnamon, oregano, tomatoes and their juice, tomato purée and remaining oil in a medium bowl. Cook on HIGH for 10–12 minutes or until the onion is soft and the sauce is slightly reduced.

3 Add the beans and season to taste with salt and pepper. Spoon half of the mixture into a gratin dish.

4 Using a serrated knife, thinly slice the aubergines and arrange half on top of the bean sauce. Repeat the layers once, ending with a layer of aubergines.

5 To make the topping, beat the eggs into the yogurt. Season generously with nutmeg and salt and pepper. Spoon evenly on top of the aubergines.

6 Cook on MEDIUM for 10–12 minutes or until the topping is set round the edge but still slightly liquid in the centre. Sprinkle with the Parmesan cheese and brown under a preheated grill, if liked. Serve with a Greek salad.

# VEGETABLE BIRYANI

### SERVES 4–6

20 ml (4 tsp) vegetable oil

seeds of 4 cardamoms

5 ml (1 level tsp) cumin seeds

4 cloves

2.5 cm (1 inch) cinnamon stick

225 g (8 oz) brown or white basmati rice

450 ml ($\frac{3}{4}$ pint) boiling vegetable stock

2 garlic cloves, skinned

2.5 cm (1 inch) piece of fresh root ginger, peeled

1 medium onion, skinned and chopped

2.5 ml ($\frac{1}{2}$ level tsp) chilli powder

5 ml (1 level tsp) coriander seeds

2.5 ml ($\frac{1}{2}$ level tsp) ground turmeric

15 ml (1 level tbsp) poppy seeds

2 medium potatoes, scrubbed and cubed

175 g (6 oz) cauliflower florets

2 medium carrots, peeled and cubed

1 large green pepper, seeded and sliced

50 g (2 oz) French beans, cut into 2.5 cm (1 inch) pieces

2 large tomatoes, roughly chopped

100 g (4 oz) fresh or frozen peas

100 g (4 oz) button mushrooms, halved

150 ml ($\frac{1}{4}$ pint) natural yogurt

30 ml (2 tbsp) chopped fresh coriander

2 green chillies, seeded and finely chopped

60 ml (4 tbsp) lemon or lime juice

onion rings and fresh coriander, to garnish

1 Put half the oil, the cardamom seeds, cumin seeds, cloves and cinnamon stick in a medium bowl. Cook on HIGH for 30 seconds. Add the rice and stir to coat in the fried spice mixture. Add the stock. Cover and cook on HIGH for 30–35 minutes if using brown rice and 10–12 minutes if using white, or until tender, stirring once and adding a little extra water if necessary. Leave to stand, covered, while cooking the spices and vegetables.

2 Put the garlic, ginger, onion, chilli powder, coriander seeds, turmeric and poppy seeds in a blender or food processor with about 15 ml (1 tbsp) water. Blend until smooth.

3 Put the remaining oil and the spice paste in a large serving dish. Cook on HIGH for 2 minutes, stirring frequently. Add the potatoes, cauliflower, carrots, green pepper and French beans. Cover and cook on HIGH for 5 minutes. Add the tomatoes, peas and mushrooms and microwave on HIGH for a further 2 minutes. Gradually add the yogurt and chopped coriander.

4 Spoon the rice evenly over the vegetable mixture. Sprinkle with the chillies and pour over the lemon juice. DO NOT STIR. Recover and cook on HIGH for 12–15 minutes or until the vegetables are tender. Fluff up the rice with a fork and garnish with onion rings and coriander. Serve immediately.

# VEGETABLE AND CHICK-PEA CASSEROLE

### SERVES 6

4 courgettes, trimmed and cut into 1 cm ($\frac{1}{2}$ inch) lengths

1 red pepper, seeded and chopped

1 green pepper, seeded and chopped

2 medium onions, skinned and roughly chopped

2 carrots, peeled and thinly sliced

225 g (8 oz) turnips, peeled and thinly sliced

1 small cauliflower, trimmed and cut into florets

4 large tomatoes, skinned, seeded and chopped

100 g (4 oz) no-soak dried apricots, cut into quarters

2 garlic cloves, skinned and crushed

425 g (15 oz) can chick-peas, drained

25 g (1 oz) almonds, blanched

5 ml (1 level tsp) ground turmeric

10 ml (2 level tsp) paprika

2.5 ml ($\frac{1}{2}$ level tsp) ground coriander

salt and pepper

600 ml (1 pint) boiling vegetable stock

chopped fresh coriander or parsley, to garnish

*1* Place all of the prepared vegetables, the apricots, the garlic, chick-peas and almonds in a large bowl and stir in the spices, the salt, pepper and stock. Cover and cook on HIGH for 8–10 minutes or until the vegetables come to the boil.

*2* Continue cooking on HIGH for a further 30–40 minutes or until the vegetables are well cooked, stirring two or three times during cooking. Serve garnished with coriander or parsley.

*Vegetable and Chick-pea Casserole*

# TWO CHEESE, SPINACH AND PINE NUT PIE

### SERVES 6

1 small onion, skinned and finely chopped

1 garlic clove, skinned and crushed

15 ml (1 tbsp) olive oil

450 g (1 lb) packet frozen spinach

225 g (8 oz) ricotta cheese

1 egg

25 g (1 oz) pine nuts

freshly grated nutmeg

salt and pepper

225 g (8 oz) Granary flour

75 g (3 oz) strong white flour

2.5 ml ($\frac{1}{2}$ level tsp) bicarbonate of soda

5 ml (1 level tsp) baking powder

300 ml ($\frac{1}{2}$ pint) thin natural yogurt or smetana

100 g (4 oz) mozzarella cheese

*1* Put the onion, garlic and oil in a large bowl. Cover and cook on HIGH for 3–4 minutes or until soft. Add the spinach. Cook on HIGH for 8–9 minutes or until the spinach is thawed. Drain and return to the bowl.

*2* Add the ricotta, egg and pine nuts, mix well and season.

*3* To make the base, put the flours, bicarbonate of soda, baking powder and salt to taste in a bowl, and mix well together. Pour in the yogurt and mix quickly to form a soft dough. Knead lightly on a floured surface then line a greased 23 cm (9 inch) flan dish.

*4* Stand on a roasting rack and cook on HIGH for 8–10 minutes or until firm.

*5* Spoon in the filling and cook on HIGH for 3 minutes. Grate the mozzarella cheese on top and cook under a hot grill until browned.

# SPECIAL OCCASIONS

## LAMB NOISETTES WITH ONION AND FRESH SAGE PURÉE

### SERVES 2

15 g (½ oz) butter or margarine

1 medium onion, skinned and finely chopped

75 ml (3 fl oz) chicken stock

2.5 ml (½ tsp) chopped fresh sage

5 ml (1 tsp) lemon juice

salt and pepper

45 ml (3 tbsp) soured cream

4 lamb noisettes, each about 4 cm (1½ inches) thick

15 ml (1 level tbsp) plain flour

15 ml (1 tbsp) vegetable oil

fresh sage, to garnish

*1* To make the purée, put the butter in a medium bowl and cook on HIGH for 30 seconds or until melted.

*2* Stir in the onion, cover and cook on HIGH for 4–6 minutes or until really soft, stirring occasionally.

*3* Stir in the stock, sage and lemon juice, re-cover and cook on HIGH for 3 minutes, stirring occasionally. Season to taste with salt and pepper. Leave to cool slightly, then add the soured cream.

*4* Heat a browning dish on HIGH for 5–8 minutes or according to manufacturer's instructions.

*5* Meanwhile, purée the onion mixture in a blender or food processor, then turn into a clean serving bowl. Set aside.

*6* Lightly coat the noisettes with the flour and season to taste with salt and pepper. Add the oil to the browning dish, then quickly add the noisettes, arranging them in a circle in the dish. Cook on HIGH for 2 minutes. Turn over and cook on HIGH for 1–2 minutes or until cooked as desired. They should still be slightly pink in the centre. Arrange on a warmed serving plate and garnish with fresh sage.

*7* Cook the onion purée on HIGH for 1–2 minutes or until hot. Adjust the seasoning if necessary. Serve with the noisettes.

## SPINACH STUFFED SADDLE OF LAMB

### SERVES 6

25 g (1 oz) butter or margarine

1 medium onion, skinned and chopped

300 g (10.6 oz) packet frozen spinach, thawed

25 g (1 oz) fresh breadcrumbs

finely grated rind and juice of $\frac{1}{2}$ lemon

salt and pepper

about 1.5 kg (3 lb) saddle of lamb, boned

30 ml (2 level tbsp) redcurrant jelly

*1* Place the butter in a small bowl and cook on HIGH for 45 seconds or until melted. Add the onion, cover and cook on HIGH for 5–7 minutes or until softened.

*2* Drain and discard all the excess liquid from the spinach, then add it to the onion with the breadcrumbs and lemon rind and juice. Season to taste with salt and pepper and mix together well.

*3* Place the meat fat side uppermost on a flat surface and score the fat with a sharp knife. Turn the meat over and spread it with the stuffing. Fold over to enclose the stuffing and sew the edges together with fine string to form a neat and even shape.

*4* Weigh the stuffed joint and calculate the cooking time at 8 minutes per 450 g (1 lb). Place the joint in a roasting bag and place it on a roasting rack. Cook on HIGH for half the cooking time. Remove from the oven and remove the meat from the roasting bag.

*5* Place the redcurrant jelly in a small bowl and cook on HIGH for 30 seconds or until melted, then brush over the lamb. Return the meat to the cooker, uncovered, and cook on HIGH for the remaining calculated time. Leave to stand for 10–15 minutes. To serve, remove the string and carve into thick slices.

## CROWN ROAST OF LAMB WITH MUSHROOM STUFFING

### SERVES 4

25 g (1 oz) butter or margarine

1 medium onion, skinned and finely chopped

100 g (4 oz) button mushrooms, chopped

finely grated rind of 1 lemon

100 g (4 oz) fresh white breadcrumbs

15 ml (1 tbsp) chopped fresh parsley

15 ml (1 tbsp) chopped fresh thyme or 5 ml (1 level tsp) dried

salt and pepper

1 egg, lightly beaten

1 crown roast lamb, prepared weight about 1.1 kg ($2\frac{1}{2}$ lb), made up of 12–14 chops

*1* Put the butter, onion and mushrooms in a medium bowl. Cover and cook on HIGH for 5–7 minutes or until the onion has softened. Mix in the lemon rind, breadcrumbs, parsley, thyme, and salt and pepper to taste. Add sufficient egg to bind the mixture.

*2* Fill the centre of the crown with the stuffing, then weigh the joint and calculate the cooking time allowing 9–11 minutes per 450 g (1 lb).

*3* Place the crown on a roasting rack in a large shallow dish. Cook on MEDIUM for the calculated time, turning the roast round halfway through cooking.

*4* Wrap the crown in kitchen foil and leave to stand for 10 minutes before serving.

## RACK OF LAMB WITH MINT AND TAHINI

### SERVES 2

about 350 g (12 oz) rack of lamb with 6 cutlets, chined

salt and pepper

paprika

freshly grated nutmeg

15 ml (1 tbsp) olive or vegetable oil

75 ml (3 fl oz) chicken stock

1 garlic clove, skinned and crushed

15 ml (1 tbsp) chopped fresh mint or 2.5 ml ($\frac{1}{2}$ level tsp) dried

pinch of ground cloves

15 ml (1 tbsp) tahini

1.25 ml ($\frac{1}{4}$ tsp) lemon juice

mint sprigs, to garnish

*1* Heat a browning dish on HIGH for 5–8 minutes or according to manufacturer's instructions.

*2* Meanwhile, slash the fat on the lamb at 1 cm ($\frac{1}{2}$ inch) intervals and season well with salt, pepper, paprika and nutmeg.

*3* Put the oil in the browning dish, then quickly add the lamb, fat side down, and cook on HIGH for 2 minutes.

*4* Turn the meat over and cook on HIGH for 5–6 minutes or until just cooked. The meat should still be pink in the centre. Transfer the meat to a warmed serving dish.

*5* Stir the chicken stock, garlic, mint and cloves into the dish and mix together, stirring, to loosen any sediment at the bottom of the dish. Stir in the tahini and lemon juice and season with salt, pepper and paprika. Cook on HIGH for 1 minute, stirring once.

*6* Slice the lamb into cutlets, spoon over the sauce and serve garnished with mint.

## SAGE AND BACON STUFFED PORK

### SERVES 6–8

about 1.8 kg (4 lb) loin of pork, boned and rinded

8 streaky bacon rashers, rinded

12 fresh sage leaves

2 garlic cloves, skinned and cut into slivers

salt and pepper

fresh sage, to garnish

*1* Place the pork, fat side uppermost, on a flat surface and remove most of the fat. Score the remaining fat with a sharp knife.

*2* Turn over the meat and lay half of the bacon, the sage and the garlic over the flesh. Season well with salt and pepper. Roll up and lay the remaining bacon on top.

*3* Secure the joint with fine string. Weigh the joint and calculate the cooking time allowing 8 minutes per 450 g (1 lb). Place on a roasting rack, bacon side down and cover with a split roasting bag. Stand in a shallow dish to catch the juices. Cook on HIGH for half of the calculated cooking time, then turn over and continue cooking for the remaining time.

*4* Wrap tightly in foil and leave to stand for 10 minutes. Serve cut into slices, garnished with fresh sage leaves.

*Sage and Bacon Stuffed Pork*

# BOEUF BOURGUIGNONNE

### SERVES 4

100 g (4 oz) streaky bacon, rinded and chopped

700 g (1½ lb) sirloin steak, trimmed and cut into 2.5 cm (1 inch) cubes

1 garlic clove, skinned and chopped

175 g (6 oz) silverskin or baby onions, skinned and left whole

100 g (4 oz) button mushrooms

5 ml (1 level tsp) dried mixed herbs

salt and pepper

15 ml (1 level tbsp) plain flour

225 ml (8 fl oz) red wine

chopped fresh parsley, to garnish

*1* Put the chopped bacon in a large casserole and cook on HIGH for 3 minutes.

*2* Add the steak, garlic, onions, mushrooms and herbs and season to taste with salt and pepper. Mix together. Sprinkle over the flour and stir in. Cook on HIGH for 1 minute, then gradually stir in the red wine.

*3* Cover and cook on HIGH for 5 minutes or until boiling. Reduce to LOW and continue cooking for 40–50 minutes or until the meat is tender, stirring occasionally. Serve garnished with chopped parsley.

# QUAIL WITH MUSHROOMS AND JUNIPER

### SERVES 2

4 quail, cleaned

15 ml (1 tbsp) olive or vegetable oil

150 ml (¼ pint) chicken stock

4 juniper berries

2.5 ml (½ level tsp) dried thyme

100 g (4 oz) button mushrooms, sliced

salt and pepper

15 ml (1 tbsp) gin

watercress, to garnish

*1* Heat a browning dish for 5–8 minutes or according to manufacturer's instructions. Meanwhile, using a rolling pin, beat each quail three or four times to flatten slightly.

*2* Add the oil to the dish, then quickly add the quail, breast side down. Cook on HIGH for 2 minutes. Turn the quail over and cook on HIGH for 1 minute.

*3* Stir in the stock, juniper berries, thyme, mushrooms, salt and pepper to taste and gin. Cook on HIGH for 6 minutes or until tender, turning the quail once during cooking.

*4* Transfer the quail to a warmed serving dish, then cook the cooking liquid on HIGH for 3 minutes or until slightly reduced. Season, if necessary, with salt and pepper, then pour over the quail. Garnish with watercress and serve immediately.

*Quail with Mushrooms and Juniper*

## CHICKEN ROULADES WITH MUSHROOMS IN CREAM

### SERVES 4

350 g (12 oz) button mushrooms

1 medium onion, skinned and finely chopped

2 celery sticks, trimmed and finely chopped

1 garlic clove, skinned and crushed

30 ml (2 tbsp) vegetable oil

50 g (2 oz) walnuts, finely chopped

25 g (1 oz) fresh breadcrumbs

finely grated rind and juice of 1 lemon

5 ml (1 level tsp) dried thyme

15 ml (1 tbsp) chopped fresh parsley

salt and pepper

4 chicken breasts, skinned and boned

25 g (1 oz) butter or margarine

15 ml (1 level tbsp) plain flour

150 ml ($\frac{1}{4}$ pint) whipping cream

50 ml (2 fl oz) dry white wine

*1* Slice 225 g (8 oz) mushrooms and set aside for the sauce. Finely chop the rest and place in a medium bowl.

*2* Add half the onion to the bowl with the celery, garlic and 15 ml (1 tbsp) oil. Cook on HIGH for 10 minutes or until the onion and celery are soft, stirring once. Stir in the walnuts, breadcrumbs, lemon rind, herbs and enough lemon juice to bind the mixture. Season to taste with salt and pepper.

*3* Place the chicken breasts between two sheets of dampened greaseproof paper or cling film and flatten them with a meat mallet or rolling pin to a thickness of 0.5 cm ($\frac{1}{4}$ inch). Spread the stuffing mixture over the pieces of chicken, roll up and secure them with wooden cocktail sticks.

*4* Place the chicken, seam side up, on a microwave roasting rack. Brush with half the remaining oil and cook on HIGH for 16 minutes or until tender. Turn the chicken over halfway through cooking and brush with the remaining oil. Cover and leave to stand.

*5* Place the butter in a large bowl and cook on HIGH for 45 seconds or until melted. Stir in the remaining onion and cook on HIGH for 5–7 minutes or until soft. Add the reserved mushrooms and continue to cook on HIGH for a further 7 minutes, stirring once.

*6* Stir in the flour and cook on HIGH for 30 seconds. Gradually stir in the cream and wine and cook on HIGH for 8 minutes or until thickened and smooth, stirring occasionally. Season to taste.

*7* Place the chicken in a shallow dish. Spoon over the sauce and cook on HIGH for 2 minutes or until heated through. Serve with boiled rice.

## CHICKEN VÉRONIQUE

### SERVES 4

50 g (2 oz) butter or margarine

50 g (2 oz) plain flour

300 ml ($\frac{1}{2}$ pint) boiling chicken stock

300 ml ($\frac{1}{2}$ pint) dry white wine

450 g (1 lb) chicken breast fillets, skinned and cut into 5 cm (2 inch) pieces

150 ml ($\frac{1}{4}$ pint) single cream

175 g (6 oz) seedless white grapes

salt and pepper

*1* Put the butter, flour, stock and wine in a large bowl and whisk together. Cook on HIGH for 6–7 minutes or until the sauce has boiled and thickened, whisking every minute.

*2* Stir in the chicken, cover and cook on HIGH for 6–7 minutes or until the chicken is tender, stirring occasionally.

3 Stir in the cream and grapes and season to taste with salt and pepper. Re-cover and cook on LOW for 4–5 minutes or until heated through. DO NOT ALLOW TO BOIL. Serve with cooked rice, if liked.

## BRAISED PHEASANT WITH FORCEMEAT BALLS

### SERVES 4

2 oven-ready pheasants, total weight about 2 kg (4 lb)

300 ml (½ pint) boiling chicken stock

1 medium onion, skinned and chopped

15 ml (1 tbsp) brandy

15 ml (1 level tbsp) cornflour

60 ml (4 level tbsp) redcurrant jelly

15 ml (1 tbsp) lemon juice

salt and pepper

*For the forcemeat balls*

225 g (8 oz) pork sausagemeat

30 ml (2 tbsp) chopped fresh parsley

salt and pepper

30 ml (2 level tbsp) toasted wheatgerm

1 Pat the pheasants dry with absorbent kitchen paper. Using poultry shears, cut each pheasant along the breastbone and backbone, so it is cut in half.

2 Place the pheasants, breast side down, in a shallow casserole. Pour in the stock and add the onion. Cover and cook on HIGH for 15 minutes.

3 Meanwhile, mix the sausagemeat and parsley together. Season to taste with salt and pepper and shape into eight balls. Roll each ball in the wheatgerm to coat all over.

4 Add the forcemeat balls to the casserole. Turn the pheasants over and cook on HIGH, uncovered, for 15 minutes or until the pheasants are tender.

5 Using a slotted spoon, transfer the pheasant and forcemeat balls to a heated serving dish. Cover loosely and keep hot.

6 Blend the brandy, cornflour, redcurrant jelly and lemon juice together and add to the pan juices. Season to taste. Microwave on HIGH for 5 minutes or until thickened and smooth, stirring occasionally.

7 Pour a little sauce over the pheasant and hand the remainder separately. Serve with game chips and green vegetables.

## NORMANDY CHICKEN WITH APPLES AND CIDER

### SERVES 2

15 ml (1 tbsp) vegetable oil

2 chicken quarters, halved

150 ml (¼ pint) dry cider

2 small eating apples

150 ml (¼ pint) double cream

salt and pepper

1 Heat a browning dish on HIGH for 5–8 minutes or according to manufacturer's instructions. Add the oil, then quickly add the chicken pieces and cook on HIGH for 3 minutes. Turn the chicken over and cook on HIGH for a further 2 minutes.

2 Add the cider and cook on HIGH for 5 minutes or until the chicken is tender, stirring occasionally.

3 Meanwhile, core the apples and cut into small wedges. Add to the chicken with the cream and salt and pepper to taste. Cook on HIGH for 3–5 minutes or until the apple is slightly softened. Serve hot.

## ANCHOVY AND GARLIC STUFFED MONKFISH

### SERVES 4

50 g (2 oz) can anchovies in olive oil

3 garlic cloves, skinned and crushed

45 ml (3 tbsp) chopped fresh parsley

finely grated rind and juice of ½ lemon

black pepper

1.4 kg (3 lb) piece of monkfish, skinned

parsley sprigs and lemon slices, to garnish

*1* Put the anchovies and their oil, the garlic, parsley, lemon rind and juice into a blender or food processor and purée until smooth. Season to taste with black pepper.

*2* Lay the fish on a large double sheet of greaseproof paper, then spread the anchovy and garlic paste over the top and the sides. Carefully roll the fish up inside the paper. Twist the ends together so that the paper is firmly wrapped around the fish. (This will ensure that the moisture is retained during cooking.)

*3* Place the fish in a large shallow dish and cook on HIGH for 12–14 minutes or until the fish flakes easily. (Open the parcel and check the fish after 12 minutes.)

*4* To serve, unwrap the fish and place on a serving platter. Pour the cooking juice around the fish, garnish with parsley and lemon slices and serve immediately.

## MONKFISH IN WHITE WINE

### SERVES 4

900 g (2 lb) monkfish, skinned and boned

25 g (1 oz) butter or margarine

1 large onion, skinned and chopped

1 garlic clove, skinned and crushed

450 g (1 lb) courgettes, trimmed and sliced

30 ml (2 level tbsp) plain flour

15 ml (1 level tbsp) paprika

150 ml (¼ pint) dry white wine

150 ml (¼ pint) fish or chicken stock

225 g (8 oz) tomatoes, skinned, seeded, and chopped

15 ml (1 tbsp) chopped fresh or dried basil

salt and pepper

*1* Cut the fish into 5 cm (2 inch) pieces.

*2* Place the butter in a large bowl and cook on HIGH for 45 seconds or until melted. Add the onion and garlic and cook on HIGH for 5–7 minutes or until soft, stirring once. Add the courgettes, cover and cook on HIGH for a further 2 minutes.

*3* Stir in the flour, paprika, wine, stock, tomatoes, basil and salt and pepper to taste. Cook on HIGH for 5 minutes or until boiling, then continue to cook on HIGH for a further 5 minutes.

*4* Add the fish, cover and cook on HIGH for 10 minutes or until the fish is tender, stirring once. Serve with sauté potatoes and a green salad.

## POACHED SALMON WITH SAUCE HOLLANDAISE

### SERVES 4

4 salmon steaks, each weighing about 225 g (8 oz)

60 ml (4 tbsp) medium dry white wine

100 g (4 oz) butter, cut into small pieces

2 egg yolks

30 ml (2 tbsp) white wine vinegar

white pepper

*1* Arrange the salmon with the thinner ends pointing towards the centre in a large shallow dish. Pour over the wine, cover and cook on HIGH for 6–8 minutes or until tender. Leave to stand, covered, while making the sauce.

*2* To make the sauce, put the butter in a large bowl and cook on HIGH for 30–60 seconds or until just melted (do not cook for any longer or the butter will be too hot and the mixture will curdle).

*3* Add the egg yolks and the vinegar and whisk together until well mixed. Cook on HIGH for 1–1½ minutes, whisking every 15 seconds until thick enough to coat the back of a spoon. Season with a little pepper.

*4* Transfer the salmon to four serving plates and serve immediately with the sauce.

## TROUT WITH ALMONDS

### SERVES 2

2 rainbow trout, each weighing about 225 g (8 oz), cleaned

salt and pepper

15 ml (1 level tbsp) plain flour

15 ml (1 tbsp) vegetable oil

25 g (1 oz) butter or margarine, cut into pieces

25 g (1 oz) flaked almonds

*1* Heat a browning dish on HIGH for 5–8 minutes or according to manufacturer's instructions.

*2* Meanwhile, wipe the trout and cut off their heads just behind the gills. Wash and dry with absorbent kitchen paper, then season inside with salt and pepper to taste. Season the flour with salt and pepper and use to coat the fish.

*3* Add the oil to the browning dish, then quickly add the fish. Cook on HIGH for 2 minutes, then turn the fish over and cook on HIGH for a further 2 minutes, or until the fish is cooked.

*4* Transfer the fish to a serving dish and keep warm.

*5* Quickly rinse and dry the browning dish, then add the butter and almonds. Cook on HIGH for 2–3 minutes or until the almonds are lightly browned, stirring occasionally. Pour the almonds and butter over the trout and serve immediately.

# Plait of Salmon and Courgettes

### SERVES 4

150 ml (¼ pint) dry white vermouth

large pinch of saffron strands

75 g (3 oz) butter or margarine

150 ml (¼ pint) double cream

3 large long courgettes, trimmed

900 g (2 lb) piece of fresh salmon, cut from the middle

salt and pepper

*1* Put the vermouth and saffron in a medium bowl and cook on HIGH for 2–3 minutes or until just boiling. Add 50 g (2 oz) butter and the cream and cook on HIGH for 4–5 minutes or until slightly thickened. Set aside while cooking the fish.

*2* Cut the courgettes lengthways into 0.5 cm (¼ inch) slices. Cut the green outer slices into thin strips and add to the sauce. You will need twelve middle slices to make the plaits. If you have more, cut them into thin strips and add to the sauce.

*3* Cut the salmon either side of the central bone to make two pieces. To remove the skin, put the fish, skin side down on a flat board. Starting at one corner of the thinner end insert a sharp knife between the skin and the flesh. Using a sawing action, carefully remove the skin, keeping the flesh in one piece. Repeat with the second piece of salmon. Discard the skin and the bone.

*4* Cut the salmon against the grain into twelve neat strips about 1.5 cm (¾ inch) wide. Cut the four thickest strips in half horizontally to make sixteen equal-sized strips.

*5* Remove the turntable from the cooker and cover with a double sheet of greaseproof paper. (If your cooker does not have a turntable, use a microwave baking sheet or a very large flat plate.)

*6* Lay four of the salmon strips side by side on the paper to make a square. Working at right angles to the salmon, take one courgette slice and weave it under and over the strips of salmon. Repeat with two more courgette slices to make a neat square of plaited salmon and courgette.

*7* Repeat with the remaining salmon and courgette to make four plaits, arranged side by side on the turntable or baking sheet.

*8* Dot with the remaining butter and cover with a sheet of greaseproof paper, folding the edges together to enclose the plaits completely.

*9* Cook on HIGH for about 5 minutes or until the fish is just cooked. Carefully remove from the cooker and arrange on four flat plates.

*10* Meanwhile, reheat the sauce on HIGH for 2–3 minutes or until hot. Season to taste with salt and pepper, then spoon around the salmon and courgette plaits. Serve immediately.

*Plait of Salmon and Courgettes*

## MEDITERRANEAN FISH STEW

### SERVES 6

25 g (1 oz) butter or margarine

2 celery sticks, trimmed and chopped

3 carrots, sliced

225 g (8 oz) baby onions, skinned

2 strips of lemon rind

2 garlic cloves, skinned and crushed

1 bouquet garni

pinch of saffron

397 g (14 oz) can tomatoes

150 ml ($\frac{1}{4}$ pint) fish or vegetable stock

150 ml ($\frac{1}{4}$ pint) dry red wine

6 small red mullet, each weighing about 175 g (6 oz), cleaned and scaled

6 conger eel steaks, each weighing about 150 g (5 oz)

225 g (8 oz) mussels, cleaned

salt and pepper

chopped fresh parsley, chopped garlic and grated lemon rind, to garnish (optional)

*1* Put the butter, celery, carrots, onions, lemon rind, garlic, bouquet garni, saffron, tomatoes with their juice, fish or vegetable stock and wine in a large bowl. Cover and cook on HIGH for 10–12 minutes or until the vegetables are almost tender, stirring occasionally.

*2* Meanwhile, remove and discard the heads from the mullet.

*3* Add the eel steaks to the stew and push down into the sauce. Lay the mullet on top. Cover and cook for 6–8 minutes or until the fish is tender, stirring once.

*4* Add the mussels, re-cover and cook on HIGH for 3 minutes or until the mussels are open. Discard any which do not open. Season generously with salt and pepper.

*5* To serve, divide the stew between six soup bowls, allowing one mullet and one eel steak per portion. Sprinkle with parsley, garlic and lemon rind, if wished, and serve immediately with French bread.

## LEAF-WRAPPED MULLET

### SERVES 4

4 red mullet, each weighing about 275 g (10 oz), cleaned and scaled

3–4 garlic cloves, skinned

45 ml (3 tbsp) olive oil

30 ml (2 tbsp) white wine vinegar

salt and pepper

8 large Swiss chard or spinach leaves, trimmed

*1* Using a sharp knife, slash the mullet three times on each side. Roughly chop the garlic and sprinkle into the slashes. Whisk the oil and vinegar together and season to taste with salt and pepper.

*2* Put the fish in a shallow dish and pour over the oil and vinegar. Leave in a cool place for 30 minutes to marinate.

*3* Remove the fish from the marinade and wrap each of them in two of the chard or spinach leaves. Return the wrapped fish to the dish containing the marinade.

*4* Cover and cook on HIGH for 6–8 minutes or until the fish is tender, rearranging once and basting with the marinade during cooking.

*5* Serve the fish in their leaf parcels, with a little of the marinade spooned over.

*Mediterranean Fish Stew*

# VEGETABLE
# ACCOMPANIMENTS

## BABY CARROTS WITH WATERCRESS AND ORANGE

### SERVES 4

bunch of watercress

450 g (1 lb) whole new carrots, scrubbed

15 g ($\frac{1}{2}$ oz) butter or margarine

60 ml (4 tbsp) orange juice

pepper

*1* Wash the watercress and reserve a few sprigs for garnish. Cut away any coarse stalks. Chop the leaves and remaining stalks.

*2* Put the watercress and carrots in a shallow dish. Dot with the butter and spoon over the orange juice. Season to taste with pepper only.

*3* Cover and cook on HIGH for 10–12 minutes or until tender. Adjust the seasoning before serving.

## OKRA WITH BABY ONIONS AND CORIANDER

### SERVES 4–6

15 ml (1 tbsp) olive oil

15 ml (1 tbsp) coriander seeds, crushed

1 garlic clove, skinned and crushed

225 g (8 oz) baby onions, skinned and halved

450 g (1 lb) okra, trimmed

60 ml (4 tbsp) vegetable stock

salt and pepper

*1* Put the oil, coriander and garlic in a serving bowl. Cook on HIGH for 2 minutes, stirring once.

*2* Add the onions, okra and stock and mix well together. Cover and cook on HIGH for 5–7 minutes or until the onions and okra are tender, stirring occasionally. Season to taste with salt and pepper and serve hot.

*Okra with Baby Onions and Coriander (top); Baby Carrots with Watercress and Orange*

## BUTTON MUSHROOMS WITH RED WINE AND CRUSHED CORIANDER

### SERVES 4–6

30 ml (2 level tbsp) coriander seeds

2 large garlic cloves, skinned and crushed

150 ml ($\frac{1}{4}$ pint) dry red wine

700 g (1$\frac{1}{2}$ lb) button mushrooms

salt and pepper

chopped fresh coriander, to garnish

*1* Crush the coriander seeds using a pestle and mortar, then put in a large bowl with the garlic and red wine. Cook on HIGH for 3 minutes or until the wine is bubbling.

*2* Add the whole mushrooms, cover and cook on HIGH for 8–10 minutes or until the mushrooms are tender, stirring occasionally. Season to taste with salt and pepper. Sprinkle generously with chopped fresh coriander. Serve hot or cold, as an accompaniment, or eat with bread to mop up the juices as a snack or light meal.

## CHERRY TOMATOES WITH PINE NUT AND BASIL DRESSING

### SERVES 2

15 ml (1 tbsp) olive or vegetable oil

25 g (1 oz) pine nuts

2.5 ml ($\frac{1}{2}$ level tsp) Dijon mustard

2.5 ml ($\frac{1}{2}$ level tsp) light soft brown sugar

salt and pepper

2.5 ml ($\frac{1}{2}$ tsp) white wine vinegar

225 g (8 oz) cherry tomatoes, halved

15 ml (1 tbsp) chopped fresh basil

*1* Put the oil and the nuts in a bowl and cook on HIGH for 2–3 minutes or until lightly browned, stirring frequently.

*2* Stir in the mustard, sugar and salt and pepper to taste and whisk together with a fork. Whisk in the vinegar.

*3* Add the tomatoes and cook on HIGH for 30 seconds–1 minute or until the tomatoes are just warm. Stir in the basil and serve immediately.

## SWEET CARROT RIBBONS WITH GINGER

### SERVES 4–6

700 g (1½ lb) large carrots, peeled

30 ml (2 tbsp) clear honey

2.5 ml (½ level tsp) Dijon mustard

25 g (1 oz) butter or margarine

1 cm (½ inch) piece of fresh root ginger, peeled and grated

*1* Using a potato peeler, slice the carrots lengthways into wafer thin strips.

*2* Put the honey, mustard, butter and ginger in a large bowl and cook on HIGH for 3 minutes, stirring once. Add the carrots and cook on HIGH for 1–2 minutes or until just hot, stirring once. Serve immediately.

## CREAMED PARSLEY

### SERVES 4

1 small onion, skinned and finely chopped

25 g (1 oz) butter or margarine

large bunch of parsley, weighing about 175 g (6 oz)

150 ml (¼ pint) double cream or Greek strained yogurt

freshly grated nutmeg

salt and pepper

*1* Put the onion and butter in a bowl, cover and cook on HIGH for 4–5 minutes or until the onion is softened.

*2* Meanwhile, trim the parsley, discarding any tough stalks and discoloured leaves, then chop finely (use a food processor to save time).

*3* Add the chopped parsley to the onion and cook on HIGH for 2–3 minutes or until the parsley is softened, stirring occasionally. Do not overcook or the parsley will lose its colour.

*4* Stir in the cream or yogurt and season generously with nutmeg, pepper and a little salt. Cook on HIGH for 1 minute or until hot, and serve immediately.

# GLAZED VEGETABLES PROVENÇAL

### SERVES 4

30 ml (2 tbsp) vegetable oil

1 garlic clove, skinned and crushed

½ red pepper, seeded and cut into strips

½ yellow pepper, seeded and cut into strips

½ green pepper, seeded and cut into strips

1 courgette, trimmed and thinly sliced

50 g (2 oz) mange-tout, trimmed

1 large tomato, skinned, seeded and cut into strips

60 ml (4 tbsp) dry white wine

salt and pepper

fresh basil, to garnish

*1* Heat a browning dish on HIGH for 5–8 minutes or according to manufacturer's instructions. Add the oil and garlic for the last 30 seconds.

*2* Add the vegetables and stir. Cook on HIGH for 2–3 minutes or until the vegetables are slightly softened.

*3* Stir in the white wine and season to taste with salt and pepper. Cook on HIGH for 1 minute. Transfer to a serving dish and garnish with fresh basil. Serve with chicken or turkey or, for a vegetarian meal, serve with boiled brown rice.

## CABBAGE IN CARAWAY CREAM

### SERVES 4

45 ml (3 tbsp) vegetable oil

15 ml (1 level tbsp) caraway seeds

450 g (1 lb) savoy cabbage, shredded

150 ml ($\frac{1}{4}$ pint) soured cream or Greek strained yogurt

10 ml (2 level tsp) Dijon mustard

salt and pepper

*1* Put the oil in a medium bowl. Lightly crush the caraway seeds and add to the oil. Cook on HIGH for 3 minutes or until the oil is very hot and the caraway seeds begin to release a fragrant aroma.

*2* Add the cabbage, stir to coat in the oil and cook on HIGH for 2–3 minutes or until the cabbage is tender but still crispy. (Cook for 1–2 minutes longer if you prefer less crispy cabbage, but do not cook until soggy.)

*3* Mix the cream or yogurt and mustard together, pour on to the cabbage and toss to coat. Cook on HIGH for 1 minute or until hot. Season generously with black pepper and a little salt and serve immediately.

*Glazed Vegetables Provençal (right); Cucumber with Onion and Tarragon (page 120)*

## BRAISED FENNEL

### SERVES 4

2 large fennel bulbs, each weighing about 450 g (1 lb)

1 bouquet garni

30 ml (2 tbsp) olive oil

salt and pepper

30 ml (2 level tbsp) freshly grated Parmesan cheese

*1* Trim the fennel, discarding any discoloured or bruised parts. Reserve any green feathery leaves for the garnish.

*2* Divide the fennel bulbs into quarters, then cut each quarter several times lengthways, leaving the root end intact. Pull the slices slightly apart to make fans. Arrange around the edge of a large shallow flameproof dish with the root ends towards the outside. Add the bouquet garni, then pour over 30 ml (2 tbsp) water and the olive oil. Cover and cook on HIGH for about 15 minutes or until the fennel is tender.

*3* Season to taste with salt and pepper, then sprinkle with the Parmesan cheese and brown under a hot grill. Chop the reserved fennel leaves and sprinkle on top of the fennel to garnish. Serve immediately.

## GRATED COURGETTES WITH POPPY SEEDS

### SERVES 4

30 ml (2 tbsp) olive oil

30 ml (2 tbsp) black poppy seeds

1 garlic clove, skinned and crushed

450 g (1 lb) courgettes, trimmed

salt and pepper

*1* Put the oil, poppy seeds and garlic in a shallow dish and cook on HIGH for 2–3 minutes or until very hot, stirring once.

*2* Meanwhile, coarsely grate the courgettes in a food processor or using a mandolin. Add to the hot oil and cook on HIGH for 2 minutes or until very hot, stirring occasionally. Season to taste with salt and pepper and serve.

## CUCUMBER WITH ONION AND TARRAGON

### SERVES 4

1 cucumber

salt and pepper

15 g (½ oz) butter or margarine

30 ml (2 tbsp) chopped fresh tarragon

1 bunch of spring onions, trimmed and sliced

fresh tarragon sprigs, to garnish

*1* Remove thin strips of skin evenly from all round the cucumber. Quarter the cucumber lengthways and cut into 5 cm (2 inch) chunks. Sprinkle liberally with salt. Leave for 20 minutes, then drain and pat dry.

*2* Put the cucumber, butter and tarragon into a large bowl and cover. Cook on HIGH for 1 minute, then add the spring onions and cook on HIGH for 2 minutes or until tender. Garnish with tarragon.

# BRUSSELS SPROUTS WITH HAZELNUT BUTTER

### SERVES 2

25 g (1 oz) hazelnuts

1 shallot or ½ small onion, skinned and finely chopped

25 g (1 oz) butter or margarine

salt and pepper

large pinch of ground cumin

225 g (8 oz) small Brussels sprouts, trimmed

*1* Spread the hazelnuts out evenly on a large flat plate and cook on HIGH for 2–3 minutes or until the skins 'pop', stirring occasionally.

*2* Rub the skins off, using a clean tea-towel, and chop the nuts finely.

*3* Put the shallot and butter in a medium bowl and cook on HIGH for 3–4 minutes or until the shallot is softened, stirring occasionally.

*4* Stir in the hazelnuts and season to taste with salt, pepper and cumin. Cook on HIGH for 1 minute, then stir in the Brussels sprouts.

*5* Cover and cook on HIGH for 4–5 minutes or until just tender, stirring occasionally.

# CELERIAC PURÉE

### SERVES 4–6

15 ml (1 tbsp) lemon juice

450 g (1 lb) celeriac

25 g (1 oz) butter or margarine

150 ml (¼ pint) single cream or Greek strained yogurt

salt and pepper

*1* Fill a medium bowl with cold water and add the lemon juice. Peel the celeriac and cut into 2.5 cm (1 inch) cubes, dropping them into the bowl of acidulated water as they are prepared, to prevent discoloration.

*2* Drain the celeriac and return to the bowl with 30 ml (2 tbsp) water. Cover and cook on HIGH for 6–7 minutes or until soft, stirring occasionally.

*3* Drain the celeriac and put in a blender or food processor with the butter and cream or yogurt. Purée until smooth, then season to taste with salt and pepper.

*4* Turn the purée into a serving dish, cover and cook on HIGH for 2–3 minutes or until hot. Garnish appropriately with fresh herbs and serve immediately.

## SPINACH WITH PINE NUTS

### SERVES 4

50 g (2 oz) pine nuts

900 g (2 lb) fresh spinach or 450 g (1 lb) frozen spinach

25 g (1 oz) butter or margarine

salt and pepper

*1* Spread the pine nuts out on a large plate and cook on HIGH for 4–5 minutes or until lightly toasted, stirring occasionally.

*2* Meanwhile, remove any tough stems from the fresh spinach, chop roughly and put in a bowl. When the nuts are toasted, cover the spinach and cook on HIGH for 8–10 minutes or until tender, stirring once. If using frozen spinach, put in a bowl, cover and cook on HIGH for 10–12 minutes or until thawed, stirring frequently. Drain thoroughly and return to the bowl.

*3* Add the pine nuts and the butter to the spinach and season to taste with salt and pepper. Cook on HIGH for 2–3 minutes or until very hot, stirring once. Transfer to a serving dish and serve immediately.

## PEPPERS COOKED WITH ONION AND TOMATO

### SERVES 2

15 ml (1 tbsp) vegetable oil

1 garlic clove, skinned and crushed

1 medium onion, skinned and thinly sliced

226 g (8 oz) can tomatoes, drained and chopped

5 ml (1 tsp) tomato purée

1 green pepper, seeded and cut into strips

1 yellow pepper, seeded and cut into strips

5 ml (1 tsp) chopped fresh oregano or 2.5 ml ($\frac{1}{2}$ level tsp) dried

salt and pepper

*1* Put the oil, garlic and onion in a medium bowl, cover and cook on HIGH for 5–7 minutes or until the onion is softened, stirring occasionally.

*2* Stir in the remaining ingredients, adding salt and pepper to taste, and cook on HIGH for 5 minutes or until the tomato has reduced to a thick pulp and the peppers are soft, stirring occasionally. Serve hot.

## CHICK-PEAS WITH TOMATOES

### SERVES 4

1 medium onion, skinned and finely chopped

1–2 garlic cloves, skinned and crushed

5 ml (1 level tsp) ground turmeric

10 ml (2 level tsp) ground coriander

10 ml (2 level tsp) ground cumin

5 ml (1 level tsp) paprika

2.5 ml ($\frac{1}{2}$ level tsp) mild chilli powder

10 ml (2 tsp) vegetable oil

4 tomatoes, skinned and roughly chopped

450 g (1 lb) cooked chick-peas or two 425 g (15 oz) cans, drained and rinsed

salt and pepper

15 ml (1 tbsp) chopped fresh mint

15 ml (1 tbsp) chopped fresh coriander

*1* Put the onion, garlic, turmeric, coriander, cumin, paprika, chilli and oil in a medium bowl. Cover and cook on HIGH for 5 minutes or until the onion is softened, stirring once.

*2* Add the tomatoes and chick-peas and mix well together. Cook on HIGH for 5 minutes or until the tomatoes are very soft, stirring occasionally.

*3* Season to taste with salt and pepper and stir in the chopped mint and coriander. Serve hot or cold.

## RED CABBAGE BRAISED WITH ORANGE

### SERVES 4–6

25 g (1 oz) butter or margarine

1 medium onion, skinned and finely chopped

450 g (1 lb) red cabbage, trimmed and very finely shredded

grated rind and juice of 2 oranges

15 ml (1 level tbsp) demerara sugar

10 ml (2 tsp) lemon juice

15 ml (1 tbsp) red wine vinegar

75 ml (3 fl oz) chicken stock

salt and pepper

*1* Put the butter in a large bowl and cook on HIGH for 45 seconds or until melted. Stir in the onion and cook on HIGH for 5–7 minutes or until softened.

*2* Add the cabbage, orange rind and juice, sugar, lemon juice, vinegar, stock and salt and pepper to taste. Stir together well.

*3* Re-cover and microwave on HIGH for 15–20 minutes or until the cabbage is tender. Serve hot.

# DEVILLED POTATOES

### SERVES 4

700 g (1½ lb) potatoes, peeled and cut into 2.5 cm (1 inch) cubes

50 g (2 oz) butter or margarine

10 ml (2 level tsp) prepared mustard

15 ml (1 tbsp) tomato purée

30 ml (2 tbsp) malt vinegar

15 ml (1 tbsp) Worcestershire sauce

salt and pepper

*1* Put the potatoes in a large bowl with 60 ml (4 tbsp) water. Cover and cook on HIGH for 10 minutes or until just tender, stirring occasionally.

*2* Drain the potatoes and return to the bowl. Add the butter to the potatoes and cook on HIGH for 45 seconds until the butter has melted.

*3* Blend the remaining ingredients together, pour over the potatoes and cook on HIGH for 1 minute or until heated through and the potatoes are evenly coated with the sauce. Serve hot or cold.

# LENTILS WITH RICE

### SERVES 8

50 g (2 oz) flaked almonds

50 g (2 oz) butter or margarine

50 g (2 oz) piece of fresh root ginger, peeled and finely chopped

1 large onion, skinned and finely chopped

2 garlic cloves, skinned and crushed

2.5 ml (½ level tsp) ground turmeric

2.5 ml (½ level tsp) chilli powder

5 ml (1 level tsp) cumin seeds

3 large tomatoes, skinned, seeded and chopped

275 g (10 oz) long grain rice

175 g (6 oz) green lentils

salt and pepper

30 ml (2 tbsp) chopped fresh coriander or parsley

750 ml (1¼ pints) boiling chicken stock

3 tomato slices and 1 coriander sprig, to garnish

*1* Place the almonds on a large plate or baking tray and cook on HIGH for 8–10 minutes, or until browned, stirring occasionally.

*2* Put the butter in a large casserole and cook on HIGH for 45 seconds or until melted.

*3* Add the ginger, onion and garlic. Cover and cook on HIGH for 5–6 minutes or until the onion softens. Stir in the spices and cook on HIGH for 2 minutes.

*4* Add the tomatoes, rice, lentils and salt and pepper to taste to the spice mixture and stir well to coat. Cook on HIGH for 3 minutes, stirring once.

*5* Add half the coriander or parsley and the stock to the casserole and stir well. Cover and cook on HIGH for about 10–12 minutes or until the rice and lentils are just tender and most of the stock has been absorbed. Using a fork, stir once during the cooking time.

6 Stir the rice and the lentils once again and cover tightly. Leave to stand for about 5 minutes or until all the liquid has been absorbed.

7 Fluff up the rice with a fork and garnish with the tomato slices and coriander. Serve immediately.

# BROCCOLI WITH LEMON

### SERVES 4

15 ml (1 tbsp) vegetable oil

1 small onion, skinned and finely chopped

1 garlic clove, skinned and crushed (optional)

700 g (1½ lb) broccoli, divided into small florets

grated rind and juice of 1 lemon

salt and pepper

1 Put the oil in a large bowl and add the onion and garlic, if using. Cover and cook on HIGH for 5–7 minutes or until softened.

2 Add the broccoli and the lemon rind and juice. Re-cover and cook on HIGH for 7–10 minutes or until the broccoli is just tender, stirring occasionally. Season to taste with salt and pepper.

# RUNNER BEANS WITH TOMATO AND ONION

### SERVES 4–6

15 ml (1 tbsp) vegetable oil

1 medium onion, skinned and finely chopped

1 garlic clove, skinned and crushed

5 large tomatoes, skinned and chopped

15 ml (1 tbsp) chopped fresh basil or parsley

salt and pepper

700 g (1½ lb) runner beans, trimmed and cut into 2.5 cm (1 inch) lengths

chopped fresh basil or parsley, to garnish

1 Put the oil in a large bowl with the onion and garlic and cook on HIGH for 5–7 minutes or until softened.

2 Stir in the tomatoes, basil or parsley and salt and pepper to taste, and cook on HIGH for 5 minutes, stirring occasionally, to make a thick purée.

3 Add the beans to the tomato mixture, cover and cook on HIGH for 12–15 minutes or until the beans are just tender, stirring occasionally. Serve sprinkled with chopped basil or parsley.

## SPICED WHEAT PEPPERS

### SERVES 4

75 g (3 oz) bulgar wheat

2 green peppers, weighing about 150 g (5 oz) each

1 yellow or red pepper, weighing about 150 g (5 oz)

50 g (2 oz) butter or margarine

2 medium onions, skinned and chopped

5 ml (1 level tsp) chilli powder

5 ml (1 level tsp) ground cumin

300 ml ($\frac{1}{2}$ pint) natural yogurt

75 g (3 oz) cucumber, peeled, halved, seeded and finely chopped

salt and pepper

chopped fresh parsley, to garnish

*1* Place the wheat in a mixing bowl and cover it with cold water. Cover the bowl and leave to stand for 1 hour.

*2* Cut each pepper in half vertically and remove the seeds. Finely chop one of the green peppers.

*3* Alternating the colours, place the halved peppers side by side in a shallow dish and add 60 ml (4 tbsp) water. Cover and cook on HIGH for 6 minutes, re-positioning the peppers three times during cooking. Remove from the oven and leave to stand while preparing the filling.

*4* Put the butter in a medium bowl and cook on HIGH for 1 minute until the butter melts, then stir in the chopped pepper, onions, chilli powder and cumin.

*5* Cover and cook on HIGH for 5–7 minutes or until the onions and pepper are soft. Add the well-drained bulgar wheat and cook on HIGH for 1 minute, stirring twice.

*6* Drain almost all of the water from the peppers. Fill the peppers with the wheat filling and cover. Cook on HIGH for 10 minutes, giving the dish a quarter turn three times during cooking.

*7* Put the yogurt and cucumber in a small bowl and cook on HIGH for 30–45 seconds or until they are hot but not boiling. Season well with salt and pepper.

*8* Sprinkle the peppers with the chopped parsley, season well with salt and pepper, and serve them with the cucumber and yogurt sauce served separately.

## STIR-FRIED VEGETABLES

### SERVES 4

15 ml (1 tbsp) vegetable oil

15 ml (1 tbsp) soy sauce

30 ml (2 tbsp) dry sherry

1 garlic clove, skinned and finely chopped

2.5 cm (1 inch) piece of fresh root ginger, peeled and grated

2 medium carrots, sliced into matchstick strips

50 g (2 oz) bean sprouts

100 g (4 oz) mange-tout, trimmed

1 red pepper, seeded and thinly sliced

4 spring onions, trimmed and chopped

$\frac{1}{2}$ head of Chinese leaves, thinly sliced

*1* Put the oil, soy sauce, sherry, garlic, ginger and carrots in a large bowl. Mix well together and cook on HIGH for 5 minutes or until the carrot is tender, stirring occasionally.

*2* Add the remaining vegetables and mix together. Cook on HIGH for 5 minutes or until the vegetables are just tender, stirring frequently. Serve hot.

*Spiced Wheat Peppers*

# WHOLE GRAIN, APRICOT AND NUT SALAD

### SERVES 3–4

225 g (8 oz) whole wheat grain

100 g (4 oz) no-soak dried apricots, roughly chopped

50 g (2 oz) Brazil nuts, roughly chopped

2 celery sticks, trimmed and chopped

4 spring onions, trimmed and chopped

60 ml (4 tbsp) olive oil

30 ml (2 tbsp) lemon juice

1 garlic clove, skinned and crushed

45 ml (3 tbsp) chopped fresh parsley

salt and pepper

*1* Put the whole wheat in a large bowl, cover with cold water and leave to soak overnight.

*2* The next day, drain the wheat and pour over enough boiling water to cover by about 2.5 cm (1 inch). Cover and cook on HIGH for 15–20 minutes or until tender.

*3* Meanwhile, put the apricots, nuts, celery and spring onions in a serving bowl. Whisk the oil and lemon juice together and stir in the garlic and parsley. Season generously with salt and pepper.

*4* When the wheat is cooked, drain and rinse with boiling water. Add to the bowl with the apricot mixture. Pour over the dressing and toss together.

*5* Cover, then leave for at least 1 hour to cool and allow the flavours to develop.

# POTATO, COURGETTE AND GARLIC BAKE

### SERVES 4–6

25 g (1 oz) butter or margarine

1 garlic clove, skinned and crushed

2 eggs

150 ml ($\frac{1}{4}$ pint) soured cream

450 g (1 lb) potatoes, peeled and grated

350 g (12 oz) courgettes, trimmed and grated

salt and pepper

*1* Grease and line the base of a 1.1 litre (2 pint) ring mould.

*2* Put the butter and garlic in a small bowl and cook on HIGH for 30 seconds.

*3* Beat the eggs in a medium bowl, then stir in the soured cream. Add the grated potatoes and courgettes and mix well together. Stir in the melted butter and garlic. Season to taste with salt and pepper.

*4* Turn the mixture into the prepared mould, cover and cook on HIGH for 15 minutes or until set.

*5* Leave the bake to stand for 5 minutes, then turn out on to a warmed serving plate. Serve sliced.

## POTATO AND LEEK RAMEKINS

### SERVES 2

1 large potato, weighing about 225 g (8 oz)

1 small leek

45 ml (3 tbsp) milk

salt and pepper

freshly grated nutmeg

1 egg yolk

15 g ($\frac{1}{2}$ oz) butter or margarine

5 ml (1 level tsp) poppy seeds

*1* Grease and line the bases of two 150 ml ($\frac{1}{4}$ pint) ramekin dishes with greaseproof paper.

*2* Prick the potato all over with a fork, place on absorbent kitchen paper and cook on HIGH for 5–6 minutes or until soft, turning over halfway through cooking.

*3* Meanwhile, finely chop the white part of the leek and slice the green part into very thin 4 cm (1$\frac{1}{2}$ inch) long strips. Wash separately and drain well.

*4* Put the white leek into a medium bowl with the milk, cover and cook on HIGH for 2–3 minutes or until very soft, stirring occasionally.

*5* Cut the potato in half, scoop out the flesh and stir into the cooked leek and milk. Mash well together and season to taste with salt, pepper and freshly grated nutmeg. Stir in the egg yolk.

*6* Spoon the mixture into the prepared ramekin dishes. Cover with a plate and cook on HIGH for 2–2$\frac{1}{2}$ minutes or until firm to the touch. Leave to stand.

*7* Meanwhile, put the butter in a small bowl with the strips of green leek and the poppy seeds. Cover and cook on HIGH for 2–3 minutes or until tender, stirring occasionally. Season to taste with salt and pepper.

*8* Turn the ramekins out on to a warmed serving plate and spoon over the leek and poppy seed mixture. Cook on HIGH for 1–2 minutes to heat through, if necessary. Serve immediately, with meat or fish.

## SIMPLE POTATO SALAD

### SERVES 4

700 g (1$\frac{1}{2}$ lb) small new potatoes, scrubbed

45 ml (3 tbsp) olive oil

15 ml (1 tbsp) white wine vinegar or lemon juice

30 ml (2 tbsp) chopped fresh herbs such as chervil, parsley or chives

salt and pepper

*1* Cut the potatoes in half and put in a medium bowl with 45 ml (3 tbsp) water. Cover and cook on HIGH for 12–14 minutes or until the potatoes are tender, stirring occasionally.

*2* While the potatoes are cooking, put the oil, vinegar, herbs and salt and pepper to taste into a small bowl and whisk thoroughly together.

*3* Drain the potatoes, then pour over the dressing and stir until all the potatoes are coated. Leave to stand for about 15 minutes to let the potatoes absorb the flavour, then serve while still warm. If preferred, make the salad in advance and, before serving, cook on HIGH for 2 minutes or until just warm.

# COOKING FOR CHILDREN

## CRISPY CHEESE AND HAM SANDWICHES

### MAKES 2 SANDWICHES

4 slices of bread

5 ml (1 level tsp) yeast extract

2 slices of cooked ham

50 g (2 oz) Cheddar cheese, grated

15 g ($\frac{1}{2}$ oz) butter or margarine

*1* Heat a browning dish on HIGH for 5–8 minutes or according to manufacturer's instructions.

*2* Meanwhile, spread the bread with the yeast extract. Top two slices with the ham and then the cheese. Place the remaining slices of bread on top to make sandwiches. Spread the butter on the outside of each sandwich.

*3* As soon as the browning dish is hot, put in the sandwiches. Cook on HIGH for 15 seconds, then quickly turn the sandwiches over and cook on HIGH for 15–20 seconds or until the cheese has almost melted.

*4* Cut in half and serve immediately.

## BACON AND EGG SCRAMBLE

### SERVES 2

4 streaky bacon rashers, rinded

4 eggs, beaten

30 ml (2 tbsp) double cream (optional)

25 g (1 oz) butter, cut into small pieces

salt and pepper

4 slices of bread, toasted

15 ml (1 tbsp) chopped fresh parsley

*1* Snip the bacon fat at intervals to prevent curling. Place on a plate and cover with absorbent kitchen paper. Cook on HIGH for 2–2$\frac{1}{2}$ minutes or until cooked, then chop roughly.

*2* Place the eggs, cream, if using, and butter in a medium bowl and season well with salt and pepper.

*3* Cook on HIGH for 1 minute, stirring well after 30 seconds. Add the bacon and cook on HIGH for a further 1–1$\frac{1}{2}$ minutes or until the eggs are just cooked, stirring frequently.

*4* Spoon the bacon and egg scramble on to toast, garnish with parsley and serve.

## TUNA FISH CAKES

SERVES 4

2 large potatoes, total weight about 350 g (12 oz)

25 g (1 oz) butter or margarine

1 small onion, skinned and finely chopped

198 g (7 oz) can tuna fish, drained and flaked

1 egg, hard-boiled and chopped (optional)

30 ml (2 tbsp) chopped fresh parsley

10 ml (2 tsp) lemon juice

salt and pepper

1 egg, beaten

100 g (4 oz) dried breadcrumbs

30 ml (2 tbsp) vegetable oil

lemon wedges, to serve

*1* Wash the potatoes thoroughly but do not peel. Prick them all over with a fork and cook on HIGH for 8–10 minutes or until soft.

*2* Put the butter in a large bowl and cook on HIGH for 45 seconds or until melted. Stir in the onion and cook on HIGH for 5–7 minutes or until softened.

*3* Cut the potatoes in half horizontally and scoop out the insides. Mash with the onion and butter. Stir in the tuna, egg (if using), parsley and lemon juice and season well with salt and pepper.

*4* Heat a browning dish on HIGH for 5–8 minutes or according to manufacturer's instructions.

*5* Meanwhile, shape the potato mixture into eight cakes and coat in the beaten egg and breadcrumbs seasoned with salt and pepper.

*6* Add the oil to the browning dish, then quickly add the fish cakes. Cook on HIGH for 2 minutes.

*7* Turn the cakes over and cook on HIGH for a further 2 minutes. Serve at once with lemon wedges.

## QUICK PIZZA

SERVES 2

226 g (8 oz) can tomatoes, well drained

10 ml (2 tsp) tomato purée

2.5 ml ($\frac{1}{2}$ level tsp) dried mixed herbs or oregano

salt and pepper

225 g (8 oz) self raising flour

60 ml (4 tbsp) vegetable oil

100 g (4 oz) Cheddar cheese, grated

a few anchovy fillets and stuffed green or black olives, to garnish

*1* Put the tomatoes in a small bowl with the tomato purée, herbs and salt and pepper to taste. Mash well with a fork.

*2* Put the flour and a pinch of salt in a mixing bowl, make a well in the centre, add the oil and 75–90 ml (5–6 tbsp) water and mix together to form a soft dough. Knead lightly on a floured surface until smooth.

*3* Roll out the dough to two 20 cm (8 inch) rounds. Lightly oil two large, flat plates and place a round of dough on each plate. Cook the dough, one piece at a time, on HIGH for 2–3 minutes, or until the surface looks puffy.

*4* Spread the mashed tomatoes over the two pieces of dough, then sprinkle them with the cheese. Garnish with anchovy fillets and olives.

*5* Reheat the pizzas, one at a time, on HIGH for 4–5 minutes. Remove from the oven and leave to stand for 3–4 minutes before serving.

# PASTA WITH BOLOGNESE SAUCE

### SERVES 2

5 ml (1 tsp) vegetable oil

1 shallot or ½ small onion, skinned and chopped

3 smoked streaky bacon rashers, rinded and chopped

1 garlic clove, skinned and crushed

225 g (8 oz) lean minced beef

1 medium carrot, peeled and grated

1 bay leaf

2.5 ml (½ level tsp) dried oregano

15 ml (1 tbsp) tomato purée

226 g (8 oz) can tomatoes

150 ml (¼ pint) dry red wine

100 ml (4 fl oz) beef stock

salt and pepper

225 g (8 oz) dried spaghetti

*1* Put the oil, shallot, bacon, garlic and beef in a medium bowl. Cook on HIGH for 5–7 minutes or until the onion is soft, and the meat has changed colour, stirring occasionally. Drain off any excess fat.

*2* Stir in the remaining ingredients, except the spaghetti, cover and cook on HIGH for 20–25 minutes or until the meat is tender and the sauce is slightly reduced. Leave to stand.

*3* Meanwhile, put the spaghetti in a large bowl and pour over 1.1 litres (2 pints) boiling water. Stir, cover and cook on HIGH for 5–6 minutes or until almost tender. Leave to stand, covered, for 5 minutes. Do not drain.

*4* Cook the sauce on HIGH for 1–2 minutes or until hot. Drain the spaghetti and turn into a warmed serving dish. Pour the sauce over and serve immediately.

# LAMB BURGERS

### SERVES 4

450 g (1 lb) lean minced lamb or beef

1 large onion, skinned and finely grated

5 ml (1 level tsp) salt

1.25 ml (¼ level tsp) cayenne pepper

30 ml (2 tbsp) vegetable oil

plain or toasted hamburger buns, to serve

tomato ketchup, to serve

*1* Mix the lamb and onion together and season to taste with salt and cayenne pepper.

*2* Divide the lamb mixture into four and shape each portion into a neat pattie about 2.5 cm (1 inch) thick.

*3* Heat a large browning dish on HIGH for 5–8 minutes or according to manufacturer's instructions.

*4* Add the oil, then quickly press two lamb burgers flat on to the hot surface and cook on HIGH for 2–3 minutes. Turn the burgers over, re-position them and cook on HIGH for a further 2–3 minutes or until cooked. Repeat with the remaining burgers.

*5* Serve the lamb burgers in plain or toasted hamburger buns, with tomato ketchup.

*Lamb Burgers*

# FRENCH BREAD PIZZA

### SERVES 2

397 g (14 oz) can tomatoes, drained

15 ml (1 tbsp) tomato purée

1 small onion, skinned and chopped

1 garlic clove, skinned and crushed

5 ml (1 level tsp) dried mixed herbs

salt and pepper

1 small French loaf

100 g (4 oz) Mozzarella or Cheddar cheese, grated

few olives and anchovy fillets (optional)

*1* Put the tomatoes, tomato purée, onion, garlic, herbs and salt and pepper to taste in a medium bowl and cook on HIGH for 5 minutes or until hot and slightly reduced.

*2* Cut the French bread in half horizontally, then cut each length in half. Place, crust side down, side by side, on a large flat serving plate.

*3* Spoon the tomato topping on to the bread and cover with the grated cheese. Arrange the olives and anchovies, if using, on top of the cheese. Cook on HIGH for 1 minute or until heated through. Serve immediately.

# CHEESE AND POTATO PIE

### SERVES 4

900 g (2 lb) potatoes, peeled and coarsely grated

1 medium onion, skinned and finely chopped

275 g (10 oz) Cheddar cheese, coarsely grated

225 g (8 oz) piece of ham, cut into 1 cm ($\frac{1}{2}$ inch) cubes

pinch of freshly grated nutmeg

salt and pepper

25 g (1 oz) butter or margarine, diced

50 g (2 oz) fresh breadcrumbs

30 ml (2 tbsp) chopped fresh parsley

green salad, to serve

*1* Pat the potatoes dry with absorbent kitchen paper and mix with the onion, cheese and ham. Season well with nutmeg and salt and pepper.

*2* Spoon the mixture into a 26.5 cm (10$\frac{1}{2}$ inch) shallow round flameproof dish and dot with the butter. Cover and cook on HIGH for 20–25 minutes or until the potato is cooked.

*3* Mix the breadcrumbs and parsley together and sprinkle evenly over the top. Place under a hot grill until golden brown. Serve hot with a green salad.

# FISH-STUFFED JACKET POTATOES

### SERVES 2–4

2 medium potatoes, weighing about 200 g (7 oz) each

225 g (8 oz) fish fillets, such as cod, haddock or coley

30 ml (2 tbsp) milk

65 g (2½ oz) cream cheese with herbs and garlic

30 ml (2 tbsp) chopped fresh mixed herbs, such as parsley, chives or dill

salt and pepper

50 g (2 oz) Cheddar cheese, grated

*1* Prick the potatoes all over with a fork, place on a piece of absorbent kitchen paper and cook on HIGH for 8–10 minutes or until tender, turning once.

*2* Put the fish in a shallow dish and pour over the milk. Cover and cook on HIGH for 2–3 minutes or until the fish flakes easily.

*3* While the fish is cooking, cut the potatoes in half and scoop out the flesh, leaving a shell about 0.5 cm (¼ inch) thick. Mash the potato with the cream cheese and the fresh herbs.

*4* When the fish is cooked, remove and discard the skin and flake the flesh. Mix the flaked fish and any milk remaining after cooking with the mashed potato. Season to taste with salt and pepper.

*5* Pile the potato mixture back into the potato skins and arrange on a plate. Cook on HIGH for 2–3 minutes or until hot.

*6* Sprinkle with the cheese and cook on HIGH for 1 minute or until melted. Serve hot with a mixed salad.

# PITTA BREAD WITH CHICKEN AND BEAN SPROUTS

### SERVES 2

1 red pepper, seeded and cut into thin strips

1 small onion, skinned and thinly sliced

1 medium carrot, peeled and grated

100 g (4 oz) cooked chicken, cut into strips

50 g (2 oz) bean sprouts

15 ml (1 tbsp) soy sauce

5 ml (1 tsp) clear honey

5 ml (1 level tsp) Dijon mustard

2 pitta breads

*1* Put all the ingredients except the pitta bread in a large bowl and mix well. Cover and cook on HIGH for 5 minutes or until the vegetables are just tender, stirring once. Set aside.

*2* Place the pitta breads on absorbent kitchen paper and heat on HIGH for 30 seconds or until just warm.

*3* Split and fill the pitta breads with the bean sprout and chicken mixture and serve.

# POPCORN

**MAKES ENOUGH FOR 2 GENEROUS SERVINGS**

15 ml (1 tbsp) vegetable oil

75 g (3 oz) popcorn

25 g (1 oz) butter

30 ml (2 tbsp) clear honey or golden syrup

2.5 ml (½ level tsp) ground cinnamon

few drops of vanilla flavouring

*1* Put the oil in a very large bowl and cook on HIGH for 1–2 minutes or until hot. Stir in the popcorn, cover and cook on HIGH for 7 minutes or until the popping stops, shaking the bowl occasionally.

*2* Put the butter, honey and cinnamon in a heatproof jug or a small bowl and cook on HIGH for 2 minutes or until the butter is melted. Mix together, then stir in the vanilla essence.

*3* Pour over the popcorn and toss to coat completely. Best eaten whilst still warm.

# BOSTON BROWNIES

**MAKES 12 SQUARES**

100 g (4 oz) plain chocolate, broken into small pieces

100 g (4 oz) butter or margarine, cut into pieces

100 g (4 oz) dark soft brown sugar

100 g (4 oz) self raising flour

10 ml (2 level tsp) cocoa powder

2 eggs

2.5 ml (½ tsp) vanilla flavouring

100 g (4 oz) walnuts, roughly chopped

*1* Grease a shallow 18 × 23 cm (7 × 9 inch) dish.

*2* Put the chocolate and butter in a large bowl. Cook on LOW for 4–5 minutes. Stir until the chocolate and butter have melted.

*3* Stir in the sugar, flour and cocoa. Add the eggs and vanilla flavouring and beat well to make a smooth batter. Stir in the walnuts.

*4* Pour the mixture into the prepared dish, stand on a roasting rack and cook on HIGH for 4–5 minutes or until well risen, firm to the touch, but still slightly moist on the surface.

*5* Leave to cool in the dish, then cut into squares before serving.

# CHOCOLATE BISCUIT CAKE

### MAKES 10 WEDGES

100 g (4 oz) plain chocolate, broken into small pieces

15 ml (1 tbsp) golden syrup

100 g (4 oz) butter or margarine, cut into small pieces

30 ml (2 tbsp) double cream

100 g (4 oz) digestive biscuits, roughly broken

25 g (1 oz) sultanas

25 g (1 oz) glacé cherries, chopped

50 g (2 oz) walnuts, roughly chopped

*1* Grease a loose-bottomed 18 cm (7 inch) flan tin.

*2* Put the chocolate in a large bowl with the syrup and the butter and cook on LOW for 4–5 minutes or until the chocolate has melted, stirring frequently. Add the remaining ingredients and mix thoroughly.

*3* Turn the mixture into the prepared flan tin and level the top. Mark lightly into ten wedges, then chill in the refrigerator for 1–2 hours or until set.

# FLAPJACKS

### MAKES 16

75 g (3 oz) butter or margarine

50 g (2 oz) light soft brown sugar

30 ml (2 tbsp) golden syrup

175 g (6 oz) porridge oats

*1* Grease a shallow 12.5 × 23 cm (5 × 9 inch) dish.

*2* Put the butter, sugar and syrup in a large bowl. Cook on HIGH for 2 minutes or until the sugar has dissolved, stirring once. Stir well, then mix in the oats.

*3* Press the mixture into the prepared dish. Stand the dish on a roasting rack and cook on HIGH for 2–3 minutes or until firm to the touch.

*4* Leave to cool slightly, then mark into sixteen bars. Allow to cool completely before turning out of the dish.

# QUEEN CAKES

### MAKES 18

100 g (4 oz) softened butter or soft tub margarine

100 g (4 oz) caster sugar

2 eggs

100 g (4 oz) self raising flour

50 g (2 oz) sultanas

30 ml (2 tbsp) milk

*1* Put the butter, sugar, eggs and flour in a large bowl and beat until smooth. Alternatively, put the ingredients in a food processor or mixer and mix until smooth. Mix in the sultanas and add the milk to make a soft dropping consistency.

*2* Arrange six double layers of paper cases in a microwave muffin tray. Fill the prepared paper cases half-full and cook on HIGH for 1 minute or until risen, but still slightly moist on the surface. Transfer to a wire rack to cool. Repeat twice with the remaining mixture.

### VARIATIONS

Replace the sultanas with one of the following: 50 g (2 oz) chopped dates; 50 g (2 oz) chopped glacé cherries; 50 g (2 oz) chocolate chips; 50 g (2 oz) chopped crystallised ginger.

# CHOCOLATE CRACKLES

### MAKES 12

225 g (8 oz) plain chocolate, broken into small pieces

15 ml (1 tbsp) golden syrup

50 g (2 oz) butter or margarine

50 g (2 oz) cornflakes or rice breakfast cereal

*1* Put the chocolate, golden syrup and butter in a medium bowl. Cook on LOW for 6–7 minutes or until the chocolate is melted.

*2* Mix together, then fold in the cornflakes or rice cereal. When well mixed, spoon into twelve paper cases or a shallow 20.5 cm (8 inch) round dish and leave to set. Store in the refrigerator.

# CAKES

## BLACK FOREST GÂTEAU

### SERVES 8–10

two 425 g (15 oz) cans black cherries

45 ml (3 tbsp) kirsch

3 eggs

175 g (6 oz) caster sugar

175 g (6 oz) self raising flour

25 g (1 oz) cocoa powder

5 ml (1 level tsp) baking powder

600 ml (1 pint) double cream

100 g (4 oz) chocolate curls

fresh or canned cherries, to decorate

1 Grease a deep 20.5 cm (8 inch) round dish and line the base with greaseproof paper.

2 Drain the cherries, reserving 45 ml (3 tbsp) juice. Put the cherries with the juice and the kirsch in a bowl and leave to macerate while making the cake.

3 Put the eggs and sugar in a large bowl and whisk until thick enough to leave a trail on the surface when the whisk is lifted.

4 Sift the flour, cocoa powder and baking powder into the mixture and lightly fold in with a metal spoon. Fold in 75 ml (5 tbsp) hot water. Pour the mixture into the prepared dish.

5 Stand the dish on a roasting rack, cover and cook on HIGH for 5–6 minutes or until

risen and a skewer inserted in the centre comes out clean.

6 Uncover and leave to stand for 5 minutes, then turn out and leave to cool on a wire rack.

7 Cut the cake horizontally into three. Place a layer on a flat plate and spoon over 30 ml (2 tbsp) of the cherry juice and kirsch mixture.

8 Whip the cream until it holds its shape and spread a little over the soaked sponge. Top with another layer of sponge and sprinkle with 30 ml (2 tbsp) of the juice and kirsch mixture. Spread with a layer of cream and cover with the cherries.

9 Place the remaining layer of sponge on top and sprinkle with the remaining kirsch and cherry juice.

10 Spread a thin layer of cream around the sides of the cake, reserving a little to decorate. Press the chocolate curls around the outside of the gâteau.

11 Spoon the remaining cream into a piping bag fitted with a large star nozzle. Pipe whirls of cream around the top edge of the gâteau. Decorate with the fresh or canned cherries.

# STRAWBERRY GÂTEAU

### SERVES 8

*For the shortbread base*

50 g (2 oz) plain flour

25 g (1 oz) ground rice

50 g (2 oz) butter or margarine

25 g (1 oz) caster sugar

*For the sponge*

175 g (6 oz) self raising flour

5 ml (1 level tsp) baking powder

175 g (6 oz) caster sugar

200 g (7 oz) softened butter or soft tub margarine

50 g (2 oz) ground rice

60 ml (4 tbsp) milk

3 eggs

*For the filling and decoration*

45 ml (3 tbsp) strawberry jam

300 ml ($\frac{1}{2}$ pint) double cream

75–100 g (3–4 oz) toasted flaked almonds

225 g (8 oz) strawberries, hulled

*1* Grease a 20.5 cm (8 inch) round loose-bottomed shallow cake dish and a 20.5 cm (8 inch) round deep cake dish. Line the base of the deep dish with greaseproof paper.

*2* To make the base, put the flour and ground rice in a bowl and rub in the butter until the mixture resembles fine breadcrumbs. Stir in the sugar and knead together to form a firm dough.

*3* Press the mixture into the shallow dish and level the surface with the back of a teaspoon. Prick all over with a fork, then cook on HIGH for 2–3 minutes or until the surface of the shortbread just puffs up all over and begins to look dry. Leave to cool.

*4* Put all the sponge ingredients in a bowl and beat until smooth. Alternatively, put all the ingredients in a food processor or mixer and mix until smooth.

*5* Pour the mixture into the deep cake dish and level the surface. Stand on a roasting rack and cook on HIGH for 6–7 minutes or until risen and a skewer inserted in the centre comes out clean. Leave to stand for 5 minutes, then turn out on to a wire rack and leave to cool.

*6* When the cake is cool, place the shortbread base on a flat serving plate and spread with the jam. Place the cake on the shortbread. Whip the cream until stiff and spread a little around the sides of the cake. Coat with the flaked almonds.

*7* Spread or pipe the remaining cream on top of the cake. Decorate with strawberries.
berries.

Clockwise from top: *Black Forest Gâteau (page 139); Strawberry Gâteau; Coffee, Rum and Hazelnut Gâteau (page 142)*

# COFFEE, RUM AND HAZELNUT GÂTEAU

### SERVES 12

175 g (6 oz) hazelnuts

4 eggs

30 ml (2 tbsp) chicory and coffee essence

100 g (4 oz) caster sugar

75 g (3 oz) self raising flour

25 g (1 oz) cornflour

45 ml (3 tbsp) sunflower oil

15–30 ml (1–2 tbsp) dark rum

*For the icing and decoration*

double quantity Continental butter cream (see right)

icing sugar, to dredge

*1* Grease a deep 20.5 cm (8 inch) round dish and line the base with greaseproof paper.

*2* Spread the hazelnuts out on a microwave baking tray and cook on HIGH for 2 minutes. Turn them on to a clean tea-towel and rub vigorously to remove the skins. Return them to the baking tray and cook on HIGH for 4–5 minutes or until lightly browned. Leave to cool, then chop roughly.

*3* Meanwhile, put the eggs, chicory and coffee essence and sugar in a large bowl and whisk with an electric whisk until very thick and creamy and the mixture leaves a trail when the whisk is lifted.

*4* Sift the flours together, then sift into the egg mixture. Fold in lightly using a metal spoon.

*5* Gradually sprinkle on the oil, one tablespoon at a time, and fold in very lightly, using the metal spoon. Pour the mixture into the prepared dish.

*6* Stand the dish on a roasting rack and cook on MEDIUM for 7–8 minutes or until well risen but still slightly moist on the surface.

Leave to stand for 10 minutes, then turn out on to a wire rack covered with a clean tea-towel and leave to cool.

*7* When the cake is cool, split it in half horizontally and sprinkle with the rum. Sandwich the cakes together with some of the butter cream and use the rest to coat the sides and top of the cake.

*8* To decorate, press the chopped hazelnuts around the sides and on top of the cake. Dredge with icing sugar.

# CONTINENTAL BUTTER CREAM

### MAKES ABOUT 300 ML (½ PINT)

The quantities given make sufficient to coat the top and sides of a 20.5 cm (8 inch) cake

15 ml (1 level tbsp) cornflour

40 g (1½ oz) caster sugar

150 ml (¼ pint) milk

1 egg yolk

75 g (3 oz) icing sugar

175 g (6 oz) butter, softened

*1* Blend the cornflour, sugar and a little of the milk together. Put the remaining milk in a medium bowl and heat on HIGH for 1–1½ minutes or until just boiling. Pour on to the cornflour mixture and stir well. Cook on HIGH for 1–1½ minutes or until thickened, stirring frequently.

*2* Cool slightly, then beat in the egg yolk and cook on HIGH for 1 minute, stirring frequently. Cover with a piece of greaseproof paper and leave until cold.

*3* Sift the icing sugar into a bowl, then add the butter and beat together. Fold in the cold custard and use as required.

# LEMON GÂTEAU SLICE

### SERVES 2

50 g (2 oz) butter or margarine, cut into pieces

50 g (2 oz) self raising flour

50 g (2 oz) light soft brown sugar

pinch of salt

1 egg, beaten

finely grated rind and juice of $\frac{1}{2}$ lemon

75 g (3 oz) low-fat soft cheese

30 ml (2 tbsp) single cream

15 ml (1 level tbsp) icing sugar

30 ml (2 tbsp) lemon curd

*1* Line the bases of two 11 × 7.5 cm ($4\frac{1}{2}$ × 3 inch), 350 ml (12 fl oz) containers with greaseproof paper.

*2* Put the butter in a medium bowl and cook on HIGH for 15 seconds or until just soft enough to beat. Stir in the flour, sugar, salt, egg and lemon rind and beat until smooth.

*3* Spoon into the prepared containers. Cover with absorbent kitchen paper and cook on HIGH for 1–2 minutes or until the cakes are risen but still look slightly moist on the surface, turning once during cooking. Leave to stand for 5 minutes, then turn out and leave to cool on a wire rack.

*4* Meanwhile, make the filling. Beat the cheese, cream and icing sugar together with half of the lemon juice.

*5* When the cakes are cool, spread one with 15 ml (1 tbsp) lemon curd. Spread half of the cream cheese mixture on top of the lemon curd, then sandwich the two cakes together. Swirl the remaining cream cheese mixture on top of the cake.

*6* Put the remaining lemon curd and the remaining lemon juice in a small bowl and cook on HIGH for 10 ·seconds or until just melted but not hot. Beat together, then drizzle on top of the cake. Cut in half to serve.

# SPICY APPLE CAKE

### MAKES 16 SLICES

450 g (1 lb) cooking apples, peeled, cored and roughly chopped

225 g (8 oz) plain wholemeal flour

10 ml (2 level tsp) baking powder

5 ml (1 level tsp) ground mixed spice

2.5 ml ($\frac{1}{2}$ level tsp) ground cinnamon

100 g (4 oz) softened butter or soft tub margarine

175 g (6 oz) light soft brown sugar

2 eggs

75 ml (5 tbsp) milk

icing sugar, to dredge

*1* Grease a 1.6 litre ($2\frac{3}{4}$ pint) ring mould and scatter a third of the apple in the base.

*2* Put the flour, baking powder, spices, butter, sugar, eggs and milk in a bowl and beat until smooth.

*3* Fold in the remaining apple then spoon the cake mixture into the ring mould and level the surface.

*4* Cook on HIGH for 8–9 minutes or until the cake is well risen, firm to the touch and no longer looks wet around the centre edge. Leave to cool in the dish, then turn out and dredge with icing sugar. Spicy Apple Cake will keep for 1–2 days in an airtight container.

# ALMOND AND CHERRY CAKE

### SERVES 10–12

275 g (10 oz) glacé cherries

65 g (2½ oz) self raising flour

225 g (8 oz) softened butter or soft tub margarine

225 g (8 oz) caster sugar

6 eggs, beaten

175 g (6 oz) ground almonds

2.5 ml (¼ tsp) almond flavouring

icing sugar, to dredge

*1* Grease a 2.3 litre (4 pint) ring mould.

*2* Dust the cherries lightly with 15 g (½ oz) of the flour and arrange them in the bottom of the ring mould.

*3* Put the butter and sugar in a large bowl and beat together until pale and fluffy. Beat in the eggs, a little at a time, adding a little of the flour if the mixture shows signs of curdling.

*4* Sift in the remaining flour. Add the almonds and almond flavouring and mix the ingredients together well.

*5* Carefully spoon the mixture on top of the cherries in the prepared dish and smooth the top.

*6* Cover and cook on HIGH for 13–14 minutes or until the cake is risen and a skewer inserted in the centre comes out clean.

*7* Uncover the cake and leave it in the dish until it is cold. Loosen around the sides of the cake with a palette knife and carefully turn it out on to a serving plate. Sift icing sugar over the top.

# CARROT CAKE

### SERVES 6–8

100 g (4 oz) softened butter or soft tub margarine

100 g (4 oz) dark soft brown sugar

2 eggs

grated rind and juice of 1 lemon

5 ml (1 level tsp) ground cinnamon

2.5 ml (½ level tsp) freshly grated nutmeg

2.5 ml (½ level tsp) ground cloves

15 g (½ oz) shredded coconut

100 g (4 oz) carrots, peeled and finely grated

40 g (1½ oz) ground almonds

100 g (4 oz) self raising wholemeal flour

*For the topping*

75 g (3 oz) full-fat soft cheese

50 g (2 oz) icing sugar

15 ml (1 tbsp) lemon juice

25 g (1 oz) walnuts, chopped

*1* Grease a 1.6 litre (2¾ pint) ring mould.

*2* Put the butter and sugar in a bowl and beat together until pale and fluffy. Add the eggs one at a time, beating well after each addition. Beat in the lemon rind and juice, spices, coconut and carrots. Fold in the ground almonds and the flour.

*3* Spoon the mixture into the prepared mould and level the surface. Cover and cook on HIGH for 10 minutes. When the cake is cooked it will shrink slightly away from the sides of the mould and be firm to the touch.

*4* Uncover and leave to stand for 10 minutes, then turn out and leave to cool on a wire rack.

*5* When the cake is completely cold, beat together the cheese, icing sugar and lemon juice and spread it evenly over the cake, then sprinkle with the walnuts.

# Marmalade Cake

### SERVES 8

100 g (4 oz) self raising flour

100 g (4 oz) softened butter or soft tub margarine

50 g (2 oz) caster sugar

2 eggs

75 ml (5 level tbsp) chunky orange marmalade

*For the orange icing*

100 g (4 oz) icing sugar

finely grated rind of 1 orange

*1* Grease a deep 20.5 cm (8 inch) round dish and line the base with greaseproof paper.

*2* Put the flour, butter, sugar, eggs and marmalade in a bowl and beat together until smooth and glossy.

*3* Spoon the mixture into the dish and level the surface. Stand on a roasting rack, cover and cook on HIGH for 5–6 minutes or until risen and a skewer inserted into the centre comes out clean.

*4* Uncover and leave to stand for 5 minutes, then turn out on to a wire rack covered with a clean tea-towel and leave to cool.

*5* When the cake is cold make the icing. Sift the icing sugar into a bowl and mix in the orange rind. Gradually add 15 ml (1 tbsp) hot water and beat together. The icing should be thick enough to coat the back of a spoon.

*6* Pour the icing over the cake letting it run down the sides. Leave until set.

# English Madeleines

### SERVES 8

100 g (4 oz) softened butter or soft tub margarine

100 g (4 oz) caster sugar

2 eggs

100 g (4 oz) self raising flour

75 ml (5 level tbsp) red jam

40 g (1½ oz) desiccated coconut

4 glacé cherries, halved, and angelica pieces, to decorate

*1* Line the bases of eight paper drinking cups with rounds of greaseproof paper.

*2* Put the butter, sugar, eggs and flour in a bowl and beat until smooth. Alternatively, put the ingredients in a food processor or mixer and mix until smooth.

*3* Divide the mixture evenly between the prepared cups. Place the cups on two flat plates, four on each plate.

*4* Cook one plate at a time on HIGH for 1½–2 minutes or until risen, but still slightly moist on the surface. Leave to stand for 1–2 minutes, then turn out and leave to cool on a wire rack.

*5* When the cakes are cold, trim the bases, if necessary, so that they stand firmly and are about the same height.

*6* Put the jam in a small bowl and cook on HIGH for 1–2 minutes until melted. Stir well.

*7* Spread the coconut out on a large plate. Spear a cake on a skewer or a fork, brush with the jam and then roll in the coconut until evenly coated. Repeat with the remaining cakes.

*8* Top each Madeleine with half a glacé cherry and small pieces of angelica. These cakes are best eaten on the day of making.

# BATTENBURG CAKE

### SERVES 8–10

175 g (6 oz) softened butter or soft tub margarine

175 g (6 oz) caster sugar

a few drops of vanilla flavouring

3 eggs, beaten

175 g (6 oz) self raising flour

30–60 ml (2–4 tbsp) milk

30 ml (2 level tbsp) cocoa powder

120 ml (8 level tbsp) apricot jam

225 g (8 oz) marzipan

caster sugar, to dredge

*1* Grease a shallow 18 × 23 cm (7 × 9 inch) dish. Divide the dish in half lengthways with a 'wall' of greaseproof paper. To make a wall of greaseproof paper, simply take a piece about 7.5 cm (3 inches) wider than the cake dish and make a 4 cm (1½ inch) pleat in the centre. Place in the dish.

*2* Put the butter or margarine, caster sugar, vanilla flavouring, eggs, flour and 30 ml (2 tbsp) milk in a bowl and beat until smooth. Alternatively, put the ingredients in a food processor or mixer and mix until smooth.

*3* Spoon half the mixture into one side of the prepared dish and level the surface.

*4* Add the cocoa powder and a little more milk, if necessary, to the remaining mixture to make a very soft dropping consistency. Spoon this into the other side of the prepared dish and level the surface. Cook on HIGH for 5–6 minutes or until the cake is well risen, but still looks slightly moist on the surface.

*5* Leave to stand for 5 minutes, then carefully turn out and leave to cool on a wire rack.

*6* Trim the two sponges to an equal size and cut each in half lengthways.

*7* Put the apricot jam in a small bowl and cook on HIGH for 1½–2 minutes or until hot, stirring frequently. Spread one side of one piece of the vanilla sponge with apricot jam and then place one piece of the chocolate sponge next to it and press the two firmly together.

*8* Spread more jam on top of the two halves and place the remaining two sponges on top, alternating the colours.

*9* Roll out the marzipan to an oblong long enough to go around the sponge cakes. Brush the marzipan with apricot jam and place the sponge cakes in the centre. Bring the marzipan up over the sides to enclose the sponges, then turn the cake over so the join is underneath.

*10* Press the marzipan firmly around the sponges to seal. Trim each end neatly. Use a small knife to decorate the top of the cake with a criss-cross pattern. Pinch the top side edges between thumb and forefinger to give a fluted edge. Dredge lightly with caster sugar and place on a serving dish.

*Battenburg Cake (top); English Madeleines (page 145)*

## CARAWAY SEED CAKE

### MAKES 12 SLICES

100 g (4 oz) softened butter or soft tub margarine

100 g (4 oz) caster sugar

2.5 ml ($\frac{1}{2}$ tsp) vanilla flavouring

2 eggs, beaten

175 g (6 oz) self raising wholemeal flour

10 ml (2 level tsp) caraway seeds

1 large orange

*For the icing*

1 quantity Glacé icing (see opposite)

*1* Grease a 1.6 litre (2$\frac{3}{4}$ pint) ring mould and line the base with a circle of greaseproof paper.

*2* Put the butter and sugar in a bowl and beat together until pale and fluffy, then beat in the vanilla flavouring. Add the eggs a little at a time, beating well after each addition.

*3* Remove the zest from the orange, avoiding any pith, and cut it into very thin strips. Set aside. Squeeze the juice of the orange into the cake mixture and beat thoroughly together.

*4* Spoon the cake mixture into the ring mould and level the surface. Cook on HIGH for 6–8 minutes or until well risen and firm to the touch but still looks slightly moist on the surface.

*5* Leave to stand for 5 minutes, then turn out on to a wire rack covered with a clean tea-towel and leave to cool.

*6* When the cake is cold, transfer to a serving plate. Make the icing and drizzle over the cake in a thin stream to make a pattern. Sprinkle with the orange shreds to decorate.

## CHOCOLATE MOUSSE CAKE

### SERVES 8

175 g (6 oz) plain chocolate, broken into small pieces

30 ml (2 tbsp) orange-flavoured liqueur

25 g (1 oz) butter or margarine

2 eggs

50 g (2 oz) caster sugar

25 g (1 oz) self raising flour

julienne strips of orange rind and chocolate curls, to decorate

*For the mousse topping*

225 g (8 oz) plain chocolate, broken into small pieces

30 ml (2 tbsp) orange-flavoured liqueur

2 eggs

*1* Grease a 20.5 cm (8 inch) round loose-bottomed cake dish.

*2* Put the chocolate, liqueur and butter for the cake in a bowl. Cook on LOW for 4–5 minutes or until soft. Stir until the chocolate has melted.

*3* Using an electric whisk, whisk the eggs and sugar together until very thick and creamy and the mixture leaves a trail when the whisk is lifted. Carefully fold in the flour, then fold in the melted chocolate mixture.

*4* Pour the mixture into the prepared dish, stand the dish on a roasting rack and cook on MEDIUM for 8–9 minutes or until risen, but still slightly moist on the surface. Leave to cool in the dish.

*5* When the cake is cool, make the mousse topping. Put the chocolate in a medium bowl and cook on LOW for 5–6 minutes or until soft. Stir until the chocolate has melted. Stir in the liqueur.

6 Separate the eggs and beat the egg yolks into the chocolate mixture. Whisk the egg whites until stiff, then carefully fold in. Pour the mousse over the sponge base and level the surface. Refrigerate overnight.

7 The next day, remove the cake carefully from the dish and put on to a serving plate. Arrange strips of orange rind and the chocolate curls around the edge of the cake to decorate.

## GLACÉ ICING

### MAKES ABOUT 100G (4 OZ)

The quantities given make sufficient to cover the top of an 18 cm (7 inch) cake or up to eighteen small cakes. To cover the top of a 20.5 cm (8 inch) cake, increase the quantities to 175 g (6 oz) icing sugar and 30 ml (2 tbsp) warm water. This will give a 175 g (6 oz) quantity of icing.

100 g (4 oz) icing sugar

15–30 ml (1–2 tbsp) warm water

Sift the icing sugar into a bowl. If you wish, add a few drops of any flavouring and gradually add the warm water. The icing should be thick enough to coat the back of a spoon. If necessary add more water or sugar to adjust the consistency. Add colouring, if liked, and use at once.

## GINGERBREAD

### SERVES 8

100 g (4 oz) butter or margarine

100 g (4 oz) black treacle

100 g (4 oz) dark soft brown sugar

150 ml ($\frac{1}{4}$ pint) milk

2 eggs

225 g (8 oz) plain wholemeal flour

5 ml (1 level tsp) ground mixed spice

10 ml (2 level tsp) ground ginger

1.25 ml ($\frac{1}{4}$ level tsp) bicarbonate of soda

30 ml (2 tbsp) stem ginger, finely chopped

1 Grease a 1.7 litre (3 pint) loaf dish and line the base with greaseproof paper.

2 Put the butter, treacle, sugar and milk in a large bowl and cook on HIGH for 4 minutes or until the butter has melted. Stir until the sugar has dissolved, then cool slightly.

3 Beat in the eggs, flour, spices, bicarbonate of soda and chopped ginger. Pour into the prepared dish and stand the dish on a roasting rack. Cover and cook on MEDIUM for 9–11 minutes or until firm to the touch and a skewer inserted in the centre comes out clean.

4 Uncover the dish and leave to stand until just warm, then turn out on to a wire rack to cool completely. Wrap in kitchen foil and store for 1–2 days before eating.

## STICKY TREACLE SPICE CAKE

### MAKES 16 SQUARES

100 g (4 oz) softened butter or soft tub margarine

100 g (4 oz) caster sugar

350 g (12 oz) black treacle

1 egg, beaten

275 g (10 oz) plain flour

7.5 ml (1½ level tsp) bicarbonate of soda

5 ml (1 level tsp) ground cinnamon

1.25 ml (¼ level tsp) ground ginger

1.25 ml (¼ level tsp) ground cloves

5 ml (1 level tsp) ground mixed spice

2.5 ml (½ level tsp) salt

*1* Grease a 23 cm (9 inch) square dish and line the base with greaseproof paper.

*2* Put the butter and sugar in a bowl and beat together until pale and fluffy, then beat in the treacle. Add the egg, a little at a time, beating well after each addition.

*3* Sift together the flour, bicarbonate of soda, ground cinnamon, ginger, cloves, mixed spice and salt, then beat into the creamed mixture alternately with 225 ml (8 fl oz) boiling water until the mixture is well blended.

*4* Pour the mixture into the prepared dish. Stand the dish on a roasting rack and cook on MEDIUM for 16–18 minutes or until the cake has slightly shrunk away from the sides, but still looks moist on the surface. Leave to cool in the dish. Cut into squares to serve.

## WALNUT AND CHOCOLATE CHIP CAKE

### MAKES 8–10 SLICES

175 g (6 oz) softened butter or soft tub margarine

100 g (4 oz) self raising white flour

50 g (2 oz) self raising wholemeal flour

100 g (4 oz) caster sugar

3 eggs

15 ml (1 tbsp) milk

50 g (2 oz) chocolate dots

50 g (2 oz) walnut halves, chopped

*For the filling and decoration*

1 quantity Butter cream (see opposite)

a few walnut halves

*1* Grease a deep 20.5 cm (8 inch) round dish and line the base with greaseproof paper.

*2* Put the butter, flours, sugar, eggs and milk in a bowl and beat until smooth. Alternatively, put all the ingredients in a food processor or mixer and mix until smooth. Stir in the chocolate dots and chopped walnuts.

*3* Pour the mixture into the prepared dish and level the surface. Stand the dish on a roasting rack, cover and cook on HIGH for 6–7 minutes or until risen and a skewer inserted in the centre comes out clean. Leave to stand for 10 minutes, then turn out and leave to cool on a wire rack.

*4* When the cake is completely cold, cut in half horizontally and sandwich together with half of the Butter cream. Spread the remainder on top and decorate the cake with walnut halves.

# BUTTER CREAM

### MAKES 250G (9OZ)

The quantities given make sufficient to coat the sides of an 18 cm (7 inch) cake, or give a topping and a filling. If you wish to coat both the sides and give a topping or filling, increase the amounts of butter and sugar to 100 g (4 oz) and 225 g (8 oz) respectively. This will make a 350 g (12 oz) quantity.

75 g (3 oz) butter

175 g (6 oz) icing sugar

a few drops of vanilla flavouring

15–30 ml (1–2 tbsp) milk or warm water

Cream the butter until soft and gradually sift and beat in the sugar, adding a few drops of vanilla flavouring and the milk or water.

# CHOCOLATE CUP CAKES

### MAKES 18

100 g (4 oz) softened butter or soft tub margarine

100 g (4 oz) caster sugar

2 eggs

75 g (3 oz) self raising flour

25 g (1 oz) cocoa powder

30 ml (2 tbsp) milk

*For the icing*

100 g (4 oz) plain chocolate, broken into small pieces

25 g (1 oz) butter or margarine

*1* Put the butter, sugar, eggs, flour, cocoa and milk in a bowl and beat until smooth. Alternatively, put all the ingredients in a food processor or mixer and mix until smooth.

*2* Put six double layers of paper cases in a microwave muffin tray. Fill the cases one-third full with the cake mixture.

*3* Cook on HIGH for 1 minute or until the cakes are risen, but still look slightly moist on the surface. Remove from the muffin tray and leave to cool on a wire rack. Repeat twice with tne remaining mixture to make eighteen cakes.

*4* When the cakes are cool, make the icing. Put the chocolate in a bowl and cook on LOW for 3–4 minutes or until melted. Add the butter and stir until melted. Quickly spoon the icing on top of the cakes to cover the surfaces completely. Leave until set.

# DARK CHOCOLATE CAKE

### SERVES 12

100 g (4 oz) plain chocolate, broken into small pieces

100 g (4 oz) softened butter or soft tub margarine

100 g (4 oz) caster sugar

100 g (4 oz) ground almonds

4 eggs, separated

50 g (2 oz) fresh brown breadcrumbs

1 quantity Apricot glaze (see right)

*For the icing*

200 g (7 oz) plain chocolate, broken into small pieces

200 ml (7 fl oz) double cream

*1* Grease a deep 25.5 cm (10 inch) round dish and line the base with greaseproof paper.

*2* Put the chocolate in a small bowl and cook on LOW for 4–5 minutes. Stir until melted.

*3* Cream the butter and sugar together until light and fluffy. Stir in the almonds, egg yolks, breadcrumbs and melted chocolate and beat until well mixed.

*4* Whisk the egg whites until stiff, and fold half into the chocolate mixture, then fold in the other half. Pour into the prepared dish and level the surface. Cook on MEDIUM for 10–11 minutes or until shrinking away from the edges and firm in the centre. Leave to cool in the dish, then turn out on to a wire rack and brush all over with the Apricot glaze.

*5* To make the icing, put the chocolate and cream in a bowl and cook on LOW for 6–7 minutes, or until the chocolate melts, stirring occasionally. Do not allow the mixture to boil.

*6* Mix well together, then pour the icing all at once on to the top of the cake, allowing it to run down the sides. Leave in a cool place, but not the refrigerator, until set. Transfer to a large flat plate to serve.

# APRICOT GLAZE

### MAKES 150 ML ($\frac{1}{4}$ PINT)

This quantity of glaze is sufficient to glaze about eight 9 cm ($3\frac{1}{2}$ inch) fruit tarts or two 20.5 cm (8 inch) fruit cakes. To make a smaller quantity, halve the ingredients and cook on HIGH for 30 seconds–1 minute or until boiling, then continue as below. This glaze may be reheated on HIGH for 1 minute if necessary.

75 ml (5 level tbsp) apricot jam

Put the jam in a small bowl and add 30 ml (2 tbsp) water. Cook on HIGH for 1–1$\frac{1}{2}$ minutes or until boiling, stirring occasionally. Sieve and use while still warm as required.

# APPLE AND BLACKCURRANT CRUMBLE

### SERVES 3–4

75 g (3 oz) butter or margarine

75 g (3 oz) plain wholemeal flour

25 g (1 oz) rolled oats

25 g (1 oz) sunflower seeds (optional)

15 g ($\frac{1}{2}$ oz) desiccated coconut

25 g (1 oz) chopped mixed nuts (optional)

25 g (1 oz) light soft brown sugar

5 ml (1 level tsp) ground cinnamon (optional)

2.5 ml ($\frac{1}{2}$ level tsp) ground mixed spice (optional)

225 g (8 oz) eating apples, cored and sliced

225 g (8 oz) blackcurrants

*1* Put the butter and flour in a bowl and rub together until the mixture resembles fine breadcrumbs. Stir in the dry ingredients and mix thoroughly together.

*2* Put the apples and blackcurrants in a 1.1 litre (2 pint) deep dish. Spoon the crumble mixture evenly over the fruit and press down lightly. Cook on HIGH for 11–12 minutes or until the fruit is tender. Serve hot or cold with yogurt, cream or custard.

# APRICOT CHEESECAKES

### SERVES 2

100 g (4 oz) Ricótta or curd cheese

1 egg yolk

30 ml (2 level tbsp) ground almonds

30 ml (2 level tbsp) caster sugar

finely grated rind of $\frac{1}{2}$ lemon

20 ml (4 tsp) brandy

400 g (14 oz) can apricot halves in natural juice

15 ml (1 level tbsp) apricot jam

mint sprigs, to decorate

*1* Put the Ricotta cheese and egg yolk in a medium bowl and beat thoroughly together. Beat in the almonds, sugar and lemon rind and gradually stir in 10 ml (2 tsp) of the brandy.

*2* Drain the apricots, reserving the juice. Finely chop one apricot half and stir into the cheese mixture.

*3* Spoon the mixture into two 150 ml ($\frac{1}{4}$ pint) ramekin dishes and level the surface. Cut two of the apricot halves crossways into thin slices and fan out. Press lightly on top of the cheesecakes.

*4* Cook on LOW for 15 minutes or until the edges are slightly shrinking away from the dish. Leave to stand for 10 minutes, then chill.

*5* Meanwhile, purée the remaining apricots and 30 ml (2 tbsp) of the juice in a blender or food processor. Pour into a small bowl and stir in the remaining brandy. Cook on HIGH for 2 minutes or until boiling. Leave to cool.

*6* To serve, unmould the cheesecakes and put onto two serving plates. Put the apricot jam in a small bowl and cook on HIGH for 30 seconds or until melted. Brush the cheesecakes with the glaze.

*7* Pour the sauce around the cheesecakes and decorate with the mint.

*Apricot Cheesecakes*

155

## KIWI UPSIDEDOWN PUDDING

### SERVES 2

25 g (1 oz) butter or margarine

25 g (1 oz) light soft brown sugar

25 g (1 oz) self raising wholemeal flour

1.25 ml ($\frac{1}{4}$ level tsp) ground mixed spice

1 egg, beaten

2 kiwi fruits, peeled

15 ml (1 tbsp) clear honey

15 ml (1 tbsp) lemon juice

*1* Line the base of a 7.5 x 11 cm (3 x 4½ inch) dish with greaseproof paper.

*2* Put the butter in a bowl and cook on HIGH for 10–15 seconds or until just soft enough to beat. Add the sugar, flour, mixed spice and egg and beat well together, using a wooden spoon, until the mixture is well blended and slightly glossy.

*3* Cut one of the kiwi fruits into thin slices and arrange in the base of the prepared dish.

*4* Chop the remaining kiwi fruit and stir into the sponge mixture. Beat well together. Spoon the mixture carefully on top of the kiwi slices and cover with a double thickness of absorbent kitchen paper.

*5* Cook on MEDIUM for 4–4½ minutes or until the cake has begun to shrink away from the sides of the dish but the surface still looks slightly moist. Leave to stand, covered, for 5 minutes, then turn out on to a serving plate.

*6* Meanwhile, put the honey and lemon juice in a ramekin dish or cup. Cook on HIGH for 15–30 seconds or until warmed through. Spoon over the pudding and serve warm.

## ALMOND-STUFFED PEACHES

### SERVES 4

4 firm ripe peaches

50 g (2 oz) ground almonds

finely grated rind of ½ orange

5 ml (1 tsp) clear honey

150 ml ($\frac{1}{4}$ pint) unsweetened orange juice

15 ml (1 tbsp) Amaretto (optional)

a few mint leaves, to decorate

*1* Cut the peaches in half and carefully ease out the stones. Make the hollows in the peaches a little deeper with a teaspoon.

*2* Finely chop the removed peach flesh and mix with the almonds, orange rind, honey and 15 ml (1 tbsp) of the orange juice.

*3* Use this mixture to stuff the peach halves, mounding the filling slightly.

*4* Place the peaches around the edge of a large shallow dish. Mix the remaining orange juice with the Amaretto, if using, and pour around the peaches.

*5* Cover and cook on HIGH for 3–5 minutes or until the peaches are tender. Leave to stand for 5 minutes, then serve warm with the juices spooned over and decorated with mint.

*Almond-stuffed Peaches*

# FRUIT KEBABS WITH YOGURT AND HONEY DIP

### SERVES 4

1 small pineapple

2 large firm peaches

1 large firm banana

2 crisp eating apples

1 small bunch of large black grapes, seeded

finely grated rind and juice of 1 large orange

60 ml (4 tbsp) brandy or orange-flavoured liqueur

50 g (2 oz) unsalted butter

200 ml (7 fl oz) natural yogurt

45 ml (3 tbsp) clear honey

fresh mint sprigs, to decorate

1 Cut the top and bottom off the pineapple. Stand the pineapple upright on a board and, using a very sharp knife, slice downwards in sections to remove the skin and 'eyes'. Cut the pineapple into quarters and remove the core. Cut the flesh into small cubes.

2 Skin and halve the peaches and remove the stones. Cut the flesh into chunks.

3 Peel the banana and then slice it into thick chunks. Quarter and core the apples but do not peel them. Cut each quarter in half cross-ways.

4 Put all the fruit together in a bowl. Mix the orange rind and juice with the brandy or liqueur, pour this over the fruit, cover and leave to marinate for at least 30 minutes.

5 Thread the fruit on to eight wooden kebab skewers. Put the butter in a small bowl and cook on LOW for 2 minutes or until melted, then brush over the kebabs.

6 Arrange the kebabs in a double layer on a roasting rack in a shallow dish. Cook on HIGH for 2 minutes, then re-position the kebabs so that the inside skewers are moved to the outside of the dish. Cook on HIGH for about 4 minutes, re-position twice more and baste with any juices in the dish. Leave the kebabs to stand for 5 minutes.

7 Whisk together the yogurt and 30 ml (2 tbsp) of the honey. Pour the mixture into a serving bowl, cover and cook on HIGH for 1 minute or until just warm, stirring occasionally. Drizzle over the remaining honey and decorate the dip with a few fresh mint sprigs.

8 Serve the fruit kebabs with the yogurt dip handed round separately.

# OSBORNE PUDDING

### SERVES 4

3 slices of wholemeal bread

25 g (1 oz) vegetable margarine

45 ml (3 level tbsp) marmalade

2 eggs

300 ml ($\frac{1}{2}$ pint) milk

freshly grated nutmeg

1 Spread the bread slices with the margarine, then with the marmalade. Cut the bread into fingers or small squares and arrange, marmalade side uppermost, in layers in a 900 ml (1$\frac{1}{2}$ pint) flameproof dish.

2 Beat the eggs together in a bowl, then blend in the milk. Pour the mixture over the bread and sprinkle a little nutmeg on top. Leave to stand for about 30 minutes so that the bread absorbs some of the liquid.

3 Cook, uncovered, on LOW for 20 minutes or until just set. Leave to stand for 5 minutes. Brown under a grill. Serve hot.

*Fruit Kebabs with Yogurt and Honey Dip*

# BLACKCURRANT JELLY WITH FRESH FRUIT

### SERVES 4

225 g (8 oz) blackcurrants, strung

finely grated rind and juice of ½ lemon

15 ml (1 level tbsp) gelatine

300 ml (½ pint) unsweetened apple juice

prepared fresh fruit in season, such as strawberries, kiwi fruit, oranges, raspberries, to serve

a few mint sprigs, to decorate (optional)

*1* Put the blackcurrants and lemon rind and juice in a medium bowl. Cook on HIGH for 5–6 minutes or until the blackcurrants are soft, stirring occasionally.

*2* Put the gelatine and half of the apple juice in a small bowl. Cook on HIGH for 1 minute or until hot but not boiling. Stir until dissolved, then stir into the blackcurrant mixture with the remaining apple juice.

*3* Pour the jelly into four 150 ml (¼ pint) wetted moulds or ramekins and chill for 3–4 hours until set.

*4* When set, turn out on to individual plates and arrange the prepared fruit attractively around the blackcurrant jellies. Decorate with mint sprigs, if wished.

# LEMON CHEESECAKE

### SERVES 6

75 g (3 oz) butter or margarine, cut into small pieces

175 g (6 oz) digestive biscuits, finely crushed

15 ml (1 level tbsp) gelatine

finely grated rind and juice of 1 lemon

225 g (8 oz) cottage cheese, sieved

150 ml ($\frac{1}{4}$ pint) soured cream

75 g (3 oz) caster sugar

2 eggs, separated

fresh fruit in season such as strawberries, sliced; black and green grapes, halved and seeded; or kiwi fruit, peeled and sliced, to decorate

*1* Put the butter in a bowl and cook on HIGH for 1–2 minutes or until melted. Mix in the biscuit crumbs. Press into the base of a 20.5 cm (8 inch) loose-bottomed or spring-release cake tin. Chill in the refrigerator for 30 minutes.

*2* Sprinkle the gelatine into 60 ml (4 tbsp) water in a small bowl and cook on HIGH for 1 minute. Stir until dissolved, then leave to cool slightly.

*3* Put the lemon rind and juice, cottage cheese, soured cream, sugar and egg yolks in a bowl and beat together. Stir in the gelatine.

*4* Whisk the egg whites until stiff and then fold lightly into the mixture. Carefully pour into the tin on top of the biscuit base and chill for several hours, preferably overnight.

*5* Remove the cheesecake from the tin and place on a flat serving plate. Decorate with fresh fruit.

*Blackcurrant Jelly with Fresh Fruit*

# FRUIT AND POLENTA PUDDING

## SERVES 6

568 ml (1 pint) milk

100 g (4 oz) cornmeal

100 g (4 oz) raisins

25 g (1 oz) butter or margarine

30 ml (2 tbsp) clear honey

a few drops of vanilla flavouring

finely grated rind and juice of 1 lemon

fresh fruit, such as star fruit, strawberries, kiwi fruit, raspberries, apricots, mangoes, kumquats, prepared and sliced

*For the glaze*

30 ml (2 tbsp) apricot jam

lemon juice

*1* Grease a 23 cm (9 inch) square dish and line the base with greaseproof paper.

*2* Put the milk in a large bowl and cook on HIGH for 4–5 minutes or until hot but not boiling. Gradually stir in the cornmeal and mix thoroughly together. Cook on HIGH for 5–6 minutes or until very thick, stirring frequently.

*3* Stir in the raisins, butter, honey, vanilla flavouring, lemon rind and juice and mix well together. Pour into the prepared dish and level the surface. Leave for 2–3 hours or until set.

*4* Turn the polenta on to a flat surface and cut into six pieces. Arrange the fruit attractively on top.

*5* To make the glaze, put the jam and a squeeze of lemon juice in a small bowl and cook on HIGH for 20–30 seconds or until the jam has melted. Brush over the fruit to glaze

# WARM TANGERINE AND KIWI FRUIT PARCELS

## SERVES 4

4 small, thin-skinned seedless tangerines

3 kiwi fruit, peeled and sliced

2 passion fruit

60 ml (4 level tbsp) fromage frais

a few drops of orange flower water (optional)

10 ml (2 tsp) clear honey (optional)

*1* Peel the tangerines and remove all pith. Carefully separate the segments to make a large flower shape, keeping the base still attached.

*2* Cut four 30.5 cm (12 inch) squares of greaseproof paper. Arrange the kiwi fruit in a small circle on each square, leaving a hole in the middle. Place a tangerine on top of each circle of kiwi fruit. Gather the paper up around the fruit to make four parcels and twist the edges together to seal.

*3* Halve the passion fruit, scoop out the seeds and mix with the fromage frais. Add a few drops of orange flower water, if using.

*4* Arrange the parcels in a circle in the cooker. Cook on HIGH for 1–2 minutes or until warm.

*5* To serve, arrange on four serving plates. Open the parcels slightly and place a spoonful of the fromage frais mixture in the centre of each. Drizzle with the honey and serve immediately while still warm.

*Fruit and Polenta Pudding*

# CHOCOLATE PECAN PIE

### MAKES 8 SLICES

*For the base*

100 g (4 oz) butter or margarine

225 g (8 oz) wholemeal digestive biscuits, finely crushed

75 g (3 oz) rolled oats

*For the filling*

100 g (4 oz) chocolate, broken into small pieces

25 g (1 oz) butter or margarine

100 g (4 oz) dark muscovado sugar

60 ml (4 tbsp) golden syrup

175 g (6 oz) pecan nuts, roughly chopped

2 eggs

*1* Grease a 20.5 cm (8 inch) fluted flan dish.

*2* Put the butter in a medium bowl and cook on HIGH for 1–1½ minutes or until melted. Stir in the crushed biscuits and oats and mix together. Press evenly over the base of the flan dish.

*3* To make the filling, put the chocolate, butter, sugar and golden syrup in a medium bowl and cook on HIGH for 1–2 minutes or until the chocolate has melted. Stir in the nuts and eggs and beat lightly together until well mixed.

*4* Pour over the biscuit base. Stand on a roasting rack and cook on MEDIUM for 10–12 minutes or until the mixture is set. Serve cold, cut into wedges, with thick yogurt or whipped cream.

# FIG AND HONEY RAMEKINS

### SERVES 4

about 20 dried figs

*For the filling*

175 g (6 oz) curd cheese

50 g (2 oz) shelled pistachio nuts, finely chopped

50 g (2 oz) no-soak dried apricots, finely chopped

15 ml (1 tbsp) clear honey

15 ml (1 tbsp) brandy

chopped shelled pistachio nuts, to decorate

*For the sauce*

60 ml (4 tbsp) clear honey

15 ml (1 tbsp) brandy

*1* Put the figs in a large bowl and pour over enough boiling water to cover. Cover and cook on HIGH for 5–7 minutes or until softened.

*2* To make the filling, put the cheese, nuts, apricots, honey and brandy in a bowl and beat together.

*3* Grease four ramekin dishes. Split the figs down one side, if necessary, to open them out flat. Use five figs to line the base and sides of each ramekin, arranging them skin side outwards. Fill each dish with the cheese mixture. Level the surface, cover and chill for at least 4 hours.

*4* When ready to serve, make the sauce. Put the honey and brandy in a small bowl and cook on HIGH for 1–1½ minutes or until just hot. To serve, turn out on to 4 plates and sprinkle with chopped pistachio nuts. Serve with the hot brandy sauce.

*Fig and Honey Ramekins*

# MICROWAVE CREAM MERINGUES

### MAKES 32

1 egg white

275–300 g (10–11 oz) icing sugar

fresh fruit in season, such as strawberries, raspberries, kiwi fruit, peaches

double cream, whipped

1 Put the egg white in a medium bowl and whisk lightly with a fork. Gradually sift in the icing sugar and mix to give a very firm, non-sticky but pliable dough.

2 Roll the mixture into small balls, about the size of walnuts. Place a sheet of grease-proof paper in the base of the cooker or on the turntable and arrange 6–8 balls of paste in a circle on the paper, spacing them well apart. Cook on HIGH for $1\frac{1}{2}$ minutes or until the paste has puffed up and formed meringue-like balls.

4 Carefully lift the cooked meringues off the paper and transfer to a wire rack to cool. Repeat three more times with the remaining fondant to make 32 meringues.

5 Just before serving, top the meringues with cream and fresh fruit.

# CHOCOLATE CREAMS

### SERVES 8

15 ml (1 level tbsp) powdered gelatine

30 ml (2 tbsp) rum or strong coffee

100 g (4 oz) plain chocolate

3 eggs, separated

pinch of salt

410 g (14½ oz) can evaporated milk

100 g (4 oz) granulated sugar

300 ml (10 fl oz) double cream

chocolate curls or rice paper flowers, to decorate

*1* Sprinkle the gelatine over the rum or coffee in a small bowl and leave to soften.

*2* Break the chocolate into a large bowl and cook on HIGH for 2 minutes or until melted. Beat in the gelatine, egg yolks, salt, evaporated milk and 50 g (2 oz) sugar.

*3* Cook on MEDIUM for 6 minutes or until thickened and smooth, stirring several times. Leave to stand at room temperature until cool. (Do not refrigerate.)

*4* Lightly whip the cream and fold half into the chocolate mixture.

*5* Whisk the egg whites until stiff and fold in the remaining sugar. Gently fold into the chocolate cream.

*6* Spoon into individual serving glasses and chill. Pipe the remaining cream on top of the chocolate creams. Decorate each dish with chocolate curls or rice paper flowers and serve at once.

*Chocolate Creams*

## LAYERED FRUIT PUDDING

### SERVES 6

*For the pastry*

100 g (4 oz) self raising white flour

100 g (4 oz) self raising wholemeal flour

15 ml (1 level tbsp) light soft brown sugar

100 g (4 oz) shredded suet

finely grated rind and juice of ½ lemon

*For the filling*

225 g (8 oz) eating apples

finely grated rind and juice of 1 lemon

225 g (8 oz) ripe plums

30–60 ml (2-4 level tbsp) light soft brown sugar

225 g (8 oz) raspberries or blackberries

*1* Grease a 1.4 litre (2½ pint) pudding basin or bowl and line the base with a circle of greaseproof paper.

*2* To make the pastry, put the flours, sugar, suet and lemon rind in a bowl, then mix with the lemon juice and about 90 ml (6 tbsp) water to make a soft, but not sticky, dough.

*3* Turn the dough on to a lightly floured surface and shape into a cylinder, wider at one end than the other. Cut into four pieces.

*4* Shape the smallest piece of pastry into a round large enough to fit the bottom of the pudding basin. Press into the bottom of the basin.

*5* Peel the apples, if liked, and remove the core. Cut into thin slices, then put in the bowl on top of the pastry. Sprinkle with the lemon rind and juice.

*6* Shape the next smallest piece of pastry into a round and place on top of the apples. Halve the plums and remove the stones and place on top of the pastry. Sprinkle with sugar to taste.

*7* Shape a third piece of pastry into a round and place on top of the plums. Spoon the raspberries or blackberries on top. Shape the remaining pastry into a round large enough to cover the berries and place on top, making sure that the pastry fits right to the edges of the bowl.

*8* Push the pastry down with your hand to compress the layers slightly and allow space for the pudding to rise during cooking.

*9* Cover and cook on HIGH for 14–15 minutes or until the top layer of pastry feels firm to the touch. Leave to stand, covered, for 5 minutes, then turn out and serve immediately with yogurt, cream or custard.

## POACHED DRIED FRUITS

### SERVES 2

150 g (5 oz) dried mixed fruit salad

300 ml (½ pint) fresh orange juice

strip of lemon rind

natural yogurt or single cream, to serve

*1* Put the dried fruit in a medium serving bowl. Pour over the orange juice and 100 ml (4 fl oz) water, then add the lemon rind. Mix well together.

*2* Cover and cook on HIGH for 8–10 minutes or until the fruits are almost tender, stirring occasionally.

*3* Leave to stand for 5 minutes, then serve warm or chilled with yogurt or cream.

# LAYERED FRUIT TERRINE

### SERVES 6–8

100 g (4 oz) self raising flour

100 g (4 oz) softened butter or soft tub margarine

100 g (4 oz) light soft brown sugar

2 eggs

30 ml (2 tbsp) milk

275 g (10 oz) curd cheese

50 g (2 oz) caster sugar

50 g (2 oz) ground almonds

almond flavouring

150 ml ($\frac{1}{4}$ pint) double cream

15 ml (1 tbsp) gelatine

30 ml (2 tbsp) lemon juice

2 kiwi fruits

225 g (8 oz) seedless white grapes

*For the sauce*

450 g (1 lb) strawberries

15 ml (1 tbsp) icing sugar

15 ml (1 tbsp) orange-flavoured liqueur (optional)

1 Grease a 1.7 litre (3 pint) loaf dish and line the base with greaseproof paper.

2 Put the flour, butter, brown sugar, eggs and milk in a bowl and beat until smooth. Pour into the prepared loaf dish. Stand the dish on a roasting rack and cook on HIGH for 4–5 minutes or until firm to the touch. Turn out and leave to cool on a wire rack.

3 Meanwhile, beat the cheese, caster sugar and ground almonds together. Flavour with a few drops of almond flavouring. Whip the cream until it just holds its shape, then fold into the cheese mixture.

4 When the sponge is cold, cut it in half horizontally and return half to the bottom of the loaf dish.

5 Put the gelatine and lemon juice in a small bowl and cook on HIGH for 30 seconds – 1 minute or until dissolved. Do not boil. Stir into the cheese mixture.

6 Spread one third of the cheese mixture on top of the sponge lining the loaf dish. Peel and slice the kiwi fruits and arrange on top. Top with half of the remaining cheese mixture and then a layer of grapes.Cover the grapes with the remaining cheese mixture.

7 Level the surface, then press the remaining piece of sponge on top. Chill in the refrigerator for 3–4 hours or until firm to the touch.

8 To make the sauce, purée the strawberries in a blender or food processor with the icing sugar and liqueur if using. Serve the terrine sliced, with the strawberry sauce.

# SAUCES

## SPINACH AND CHEESE SAUCE

**MAKES ABOUT 450 ML (¾ PINT)**

15 ml (1 tbsp) vegetable oil

1 garlic clove, skinned and crushed

1 small onion, skinned and chopped

450 g (1 lb) fresh spinach, washed, trimmed and chopped, or a 226 g (8 oz) packet frozen spinach

100 g (4 oz) cream cheese

freshly grated nutmeg

salt and pepper

*1* Put the oil, garlic and onion in a medium bowl. Cover and cook on HIGH for 3–4 minutes or until softened.

*2* Stir in the spinach. If using fresh, cover and cook on HIGH for 3–4 minutes or until the spinach is just cooked. If using frozen spinach, cook on HIGH for 8–9 minutes or until thawed. Drain.

*3* Put the spinach in a blender or food processor and chop roughly. Add the cheese and purée until smooth. Season generously with nutmeg and salt and pepper.

*4* Return to the bowl and cook on HIGH for 2–3 minutes or until hot. Serve with pasta.

## CREAM AND MUSHROOM SAUCE

**MAKES ABOUT 300 ML (½ PINT)**

15 g (½ oz) butter or margarine

100 g (4 oz) button mushrooms, sliced

1 garlic clove, skinned and crushed (optional)

45 ml (3 tbsp) dry white wine or vegetable stock

150 ml (¼ pint) double cream

salt and pepper

*1* Put the butter, mushrooms and garlic, if using, in a medium bowl and cook on HIGH for 2–3 minutes or until the mushrooms are softened.

*2* Add the wine or stock and cook on HIGH for 2 minutes or until boiling.

*3* Add the cream and season generously with black pepper and a little salt. Cook on HIGH for 3 minutes or until slightly reduced, stirring occasionally. Serve hot.

# ROASTED NUT AND CREAM SAUCE

**MAKES ABOUT 300 ML (½ PINT)**

100 g (4 oz) hazelnuts, almonds, walnuts, cashew nuts or pecan nuts

150 ml (¼ pint) dry white wine or vegetable stock

150 ml (¼ pint) double cream or Greek strained yogurt

ground mace

salt and pepper

*1* Spread the nuts out on a large plate and cook on HIGH for 5 minutes or until lightly browned. If using hazelnuts, cook for only 30 seconds, then tip the nuts on to a clean tea-towel and rub off the loose brown skin. Return the nuts to the cooker and cook on HIGH for a further 6–10 minutes or until lightly browned, stirring frequently. Chop finely.

*2* Put the wine or stock in a medium bowl and cook on HIGH for 3–4 minutes or until boiling. If using wine, cook for a further 2 minutes. Add the nuts and the cream and season to taste with ground mace and salt and pepper.

*3* Cook on HIGH for 3–4 minutes or until boiling and slightly reduced. Serve hot or warm.

# CURRY SAUCE

**SERVES 6**

50 g (2 oz) butter or margarine, diced

1 medium onion, skinned and finely chopped

1 garlic clove, skinned and crushed

2.5 cm (1 inch) piece of fresh root ginger, peeled and finely chopped

10 ml (2 level tsp) ground turmeric

10 ml (2 level tsp) ground coriander

10 ml (2 level tsp) ground cumin

10 ml (2 level tsp) paprika

1.25 ml (¼ level tsp) chilli powder

45 ml (3 level tbsp) plain flour

450 ml (¾ pint) boiling beef or chicken stock

30 ml (2 level tbsp) mango or apple chutney

salt and pepper

*1* Put the butter in a medium bowl and cook on HIGH for 1 minute or until melted.

*2* Stir in the onion, garlic and ginger and cook on HIGH for 5–7 minutes or until softened.

*3* Stir in the spices and flour and cook on HIGH for 30 seconds. Gradually stir in the stock. Cook on HIGH for 4–5 minutes or until the sauce is boiling and thickened, whisking every minute.

*4* Add the chutney and season to taste with salt and pepper. Cook on HIGH for 30 seconds to reheat.

## TOMATO AND OLIVE SAUCE

**MAKES ABOUT 450 ML (¾ PINT)**

25 g (1 oz) butter or margarine

1 large onion, skinned and finely chopped

1 celery stick, trimmed and finely chopped

1 garlic clove, skinned and crushed

450 g (1 lb) ripe tomatoes, skinned, seeded and chopped, or 397 g (14 oz) can tomatoes

150 ml (¼ pint) chicken stock

15 ml (1 tbsp) tomato purée

5 ml (1 level tsp) granulated sugar

salt and pepper

50 g (2 oz) stuffed olives, sliced

*1* Place the butter in a large bowl and cook on HIGH for 45 seconds or until melted. Add the onion, celery and garlic and cook on HIGH for 5–7 minutes or until the vegetables are soft.

*2* Stir in the chopped fresh tomatoes or canned tomatoes with juice, the stock, tomato purée and sugar. Season to taste with salt and pepper. Cook on HIGH for 10 minutes or until the sauce has thickened, stirring once or twice during cooking.

*3* Leave to cool slightly, then purée in a blender or food processor. Pour the sauce back into the bowl and add the olives. Reheat on HIGH for 2 minutes and check seasoning. Serve hot with chops, hamburgers, over vegetables or with pasta.

**VARIATION**

Fresh Tomato Sauce: omit the olives and celery. Sieve the sauce after puréeing in step 3.

## TUNA AND ONION SAUCE

**SERVES 4**

25 g (1 oz) butter or margarine

1 large onion, skinned and finely chopped

198 g (7 oz) can tuna, drained and flaked

60 ml (4 tbsp) chicken stock

45 ml (3 tbsp) soured cream

2.5 ml (½ level tsp) paprika

salt and pepper

*1* Put the butter in a medium bowl and cook on HIGH for 45 seconds or until melted. Stir in the onion and cook on HIGH for 5–7 minutes or until softened.

*2* Add the tuna, stock and soured cream and stir gently. Cook on HIGH for 3 minutes or until hot. Add the paprika and season to taste with salt and pepper. Serve with pasta and Parmesan cheese or freshly cooked vegetables, such as French beans.

*Tomato and Olive Sauce*

# BOLOGNESE SAUCE

### MAKES ENOUGH FOR 4 SERVINGS OF PASTA

25 g (1 oz) butter or margarine

45 ml (3 tbsp) vegetable oil

2 streaky bacon rashers, rinded and finely chopped

1 small onion, skinned and finely chopped

1 small carrot, peeled and finely chopped

1 small celery stick, trimmed and finely chopped

1 garlic clove, skinned and crushed

1 bay leaf

15 ml (1 tbsp) tomato purée

225 g (8 oz) lean minced beef

10 ml (2 tsp) chopped mixed fresh herbs or 5 ml (1 level tsp) dried

150 ml (¼ pint) dry red wine

150 ml (¼ pint) beef stock

salt and pepper

*1* Put the butter and oil in a large bowl and cook on HIGH for 1 minute. Stir in the bacon, vegetables and garlic and mix well. Cover and cook on HIGH for 6–8 minutes or until the vegetables begin to soften.

*2* Add the bay leaf to the vegetables and stir in the tomato purée and minced beef. Cook on HIGH for 3–4 minutes, stirring two or three times to break up the beef.

*3* Add the herbs, wine and stock and stir well to ensure that the meat is free of lumps. Cover and cook on HIGH for 4–5 minutes or until boiling, then continue to cook on HIGH for 12–15 minutes or until the sauce is thick, stirring frequently. Season well with salt and pepper. Serve hot.

# PEAR AND LEEK SAUCE

### MAKES ABOUT 450 ML (¾ PINT)

450 g (1 lb) hard pears

450 g (1 lb) leeks

1 garlic clove, skinned and crushed

150 ml (¼ pint) vegetable stock

10 ml (2 level tsp) light soft brown sugar

50 g (2 oz) butter or margarine

salt and pepper

*1* Peel, core and roughly chop the pears. Trim and thinly slice the leeks. Put the pears, leeks, garlic, stock and sugar in a large bowl. Cover and cook on HIGH for 12–14 minutes or until really soft.

*2* Put the sauce in a blender or food processor with the butter and purée until smooth. Season to taste with salt and pepper. Serve hot.

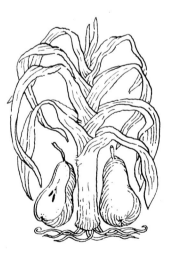

## CUCUMBER SAUCE

MAKES ABOUT 300 ML (½ PINT)

50 g (2 oz) butter or margarine

1 large cucumber, peeled, seeded and finely chopped

5 ml (1 level tsp) plain flour

15 ml (1 tbsp) white wine vinegar

150 ml (¼ pint) fish stock or water

10 ml (2 tsp) finely chopped fresh tarragon

salt and pepper

*1* Put the butter in a large bowl and cook on HIGH for 1 minute or until melted.

*2* Stir the cucumber into the butter. Cover and cook on HIGH for 6 minutes or until the cucumber is very soft, stirring two or three times.

*3* Blend the flour with the vinegar and stir in the fish stock or water. Stir this into the cucumber and add the tarragon. Cook on HIGH for 3–4 minutes or until the sauce is boiling, stirring frequently. Season well with salt and pepper.

## HAZELNUT AND CORIANDER PESTO

MAKES ABOUT 300 ML (½ PINT) – ENOUGH FOR 4-6 SERVINGS OF PASTA

75 g (3 oz) hazelnuts

1 large bunch of coriander, weighing about 100 g (4 oz)

2–3 garlic cloves, skinned and crushed

finely grated rind and juice of ½ lemon

about 150 ml (¼ pint) olive, sunflower or corn oil

salt and pepper

*1* Spread the hazelnuts out on a large plate and cook on HIGH for 4–5 minutes or until lightly toasted. Tip into a blender or food processor

*2* Trim the stalks from the coriander and discard. Put the leaves into the blender with the garlic and the lemon rind and juice. Process until finely chopped, then with the machine still running, gradually add the oil in a thin, steady stream until you have a fairly thick sauce-like consistency.

*3* Season with black pepper and a little salt. Turn into a bowl or jar, cover tightly, and use as required. Store in the refrigerator for 1–2 weeks.

## BREAD SAUCE

**MAKES ABOUT 450 ML (¾ PINT)**

6 cloves

1 medium onion, skinned

4 black peppercorns

a few blades of mace

450 ml (¾ pint) milk

25 g (1 oz) butter or margarine

100 g (4 oz) fresh breadcrumbs

salt and pepper

30 ml (2 tbsp) single cream (optional)

*1* Stick the cloves into the onion and place in a medium bowl together with the peppercorns and mace. Pour in the milk. Cook on HIGH for 5 minutes or until the milk is hot, stirring occasionally. Cover and leave to infuse for at least 30 minutes.

*2* Discard the peppercorns and mace and add the butter and breadcrumbs. Mix well, cover and cook on HIGH for 3 minutes or until the sauce has thickened, whisking every minute. Remove the onion, season to taste with salt and pepper and stir in the cream, if using. Serve hot or warm.

## HARISSA SAUCE

**MAKES ABOUT 300 ML (½ PINT)**

15 ml (1 tbsp) vegetable oil

1 large red pepper, seeded and chopped

2 red chillies, seeded and chopped

2 garlic cloves, skinned and crushed

15 ml (1 level tbsp) ground coriander

5 ml (1 level tsp) ground caraway

salt and pepper

*1* Put all the ingredients in a medium bowl and mix well together. Cover and cook on HIGH for 8–10 minutes or until the pepper is really soft.

*2* Add 300 ml (½ pint) water, re-cover and cook on HIGH for 3–4 minutes or until the water is boiling.

*3* Rub through a sieve or purée in a blender or food processor until smooth. Season to taste with salt and pepper. Reheat on HIGH for 2–3 minutes or serve cold.

## PEANUT SAUCE

**MAKES ABOUT 450 ML (¾ PINT)**

90 ml (6 level tbsp) crunchy peanut butter

75 g (3 oz) creamed coconut, crumbled

300 ml (½ pint) water

20 ml (4 tsp) lemon juice

15 ml (1 tbsp) light soft brown sugar

2.5–5 ml (½–1 level tsp) chilli powder

15 ml (1 tbsp) tomato purée

1 garlic clove, skinned and crushed

10 ml (2 tsp) soy sauce

salt and pepper

*1* Put all the ingredients in a medium bowl and stir together well. Cover and cook on HIGH for 6–8 minutes or until the sauce is boiling and thickened, stirring frequently.

*2* Reduce the setting and cook the sauce on LOW for 5 minutes or until the sauce thickens, stirring two or three times during cooking. Serve hot with roast chicken or pork, or with chicken or meat kebabs.

## EGG CUSTARD SAUCE

**MAKES ABOUT 300 ML (½ PINT)**

300 ml (½ pint) milk

2 eggs

15 ml (1 level tbsp) granulated sugar

a few drops of vanilla flavouring

*1* Pour the milk into a large measuring jug and cook on HIGH for 2 minutes or until hot.

*2* Lightly whisk the eggs, sugar and vanilla flavouring together in a medium bowl. Add the heated milk and mix well.

*3* Cook on HIGH for 1 minute, then cook on LOW for 4½ minutes or until the custard thinly coats the back of a spoon, whisking several times during cooking. This sauce thickens slightly on cooling. Serve hot or cold.

## GOOSEBERRY SAUCE

**SERVES 2**

175 g (6 oz) gooseberries, topped and tailed

15 ml (1 level tbsp) caster sugar

15 g (½ oz) butter or margarine

salt and pepper

freshly grated nutmeg

*1* Put the gooseberries, sugar, butter and 45 ml (3 tbsp) water in a medium bowl. Cover and cook on HIGH for 4–5 minutes or until the gooseberries are softened, stirring once.

*2* Purée in a blender or food processor, then return to the rinsed-out bowl. Season well with pepper and nutmeg and add a little salt.

*3* Before serving, reheat the sauce on HIGH for 2 minutes or until hot.

# HOT RASPBERRY SAUCE

MAKES ABOUT 150 ML (¼ PINT)

225 g (8 oz) raspberries

45 ml (3 level tbsp) redcurrant jelly

15 ml (1 level tbsp) caster sugar

10 ml (2 level tsp) cornflour

5 ml (1 tsp) lemon juice

*1* Rub the raspberries through a nylon sieve into a medium bowl. Add the redcurrant jelly and caster sugar. Cook on HIGH for 2 minutes. Remove from the cooker and stir until the jelly has melted and the sugar has dissolved.

*2* Blend the cornflour to a paste with 15 ml (1 tbsp) water and stir into the raspberry mixture. Cook on HIGH for 2 minutes or until thickened, whisking every 30 seconds. Stir in the lemon juice. Serve hot with steamed pudding, or warm with ice cream.

# CHOCOLATE FUDGE SAUCE

MAKES ABOUT 300 ML (½ PINT)

75 ml (5 tbsp) single cream

25 g (1 oz) cocoa powder

100 g (4 oz) caster sugar

175 g (6 oz) golden syrup

25 g (1 oz) butter or margarine

pinch of salt

2.5 ml (½ tsp) vanilla flavouring

*1* Put all the ingredients, except the vanilla flavouring, in a medium bowl and stir together well.

*2* Cover and cook on HIGH for 5 minutes or until boiling, stirring frequently.

*3* Stir the vanilla flavouring into the sauce and allow to cool slightly before serving with ice cream or other desserts.

# PRESERVES

## CRUSHED STRAWBERRY JAM

**MAKES 700 G (1½ LB)**

450 g (1 lb) strawberries, hulled

45 ml (3 tbsp) lemon juice

450 g (1 lb) granulated sugar

knob of butter

*1* Put the strawberries in a large heatproof bowl with the lemon juice. Cover and cook on HIGH for 5 minutes or until the strawberries are soft, stirring frequently.

*2* Lightly crush the strawberries with a potato masher. Add the sugar and stir well. Cook, uncovered, on LOW for 15 minutes or until the sugar has dissolved, stirring frequently. Cook on HIGH for a further 20–25 minutes or until setting point is reached. Stir the butter into the jam.

*3* Allow the jam to cool slightly, then pour into hot sterilised jars, cover and label.

## GOOSEBERRY JAM

**MAKES ABOUT 900 G (2 LB)**

700 g (1½ lb) gooseberries

700 g (1½ lb) granulated sugar

knob of butter

*1* Put the gooseberries in a large heatproof bowl with 150 ml (¼ pint) water. Cover and cook on HIGH for 8–10 minutes or until the gooseberries are soft, stirring frequently.

*2* Stir in the sugar and cook on HIGH for 2 minutes or until dissolved. Cook, uncovered, on HIGH for 20 minutes or until setting point is reached. Stir in the butter.

*3* Pour the jam into hot sterilised jars, cover and label.

# DRIED APRICOT JAM

### MAKES ABOUT 900 G (2 LB)

225 g (8 oz) no-soak dried apricots, roughly chopped

45 ml (3 tbsp) lemon juice

450 g (1 lb) granulated sugar

25 g (1 oz) split blanched almonds

*1* Put the apricots, lemon juice and 600 ml (1 pint) boiling water in a large heatproof bowl. Cover and cook on HIGH for 15 minutes, stirring occasionally.

*2* Stir in the sugar. Cook, uncovered, on HIGH for 2 minutes or until the sugar has dissolved. Cook on HIGH for a further 12 minutes or until setting point is reached. Stir several times during cooking. Stir in the almonds.

*3* Pour the jam into hot sterilised jars, cover and label.

# BLACKBERRY JAM

### MAKES ABOUT 700 G (1½ LB)

700 g (1½ lb) blackberries

45 ml (3 tbsp) lemon juice

700 g (1½ lb) granulated sugar

knob of butter

*1* Put the blackberries and lemon juice in a large heatproof bowl. Cover and cook on HIGH for 5 minutes or until the blackberries are soft, stirring occasionally.

*2* Stir in the sugar and cook on HIGH for 2 minutes or until the sugar has dissolved, stirring frequently. Cook on HIGH for a further 15 minutes or until setting point is reached. Stir the butter into the jam.

*3* Pour the jam into hot sterilised jars, cover and label.

# ORANGE MARMALADE

MAKES ABOUT 1.1 KG (2½ LB)

900 g (2 lb) Seville oranges

juice of 2 lemons

900 g (2 lb) granulated sugar

knob of butter

*1* Pare the oranges thinly, avoiding the white pith. Shred or chop the rind and set aside.

*2* Put the fruit pith, flesh and pips in a food processor and chop until the pips are broken.

*3* Put the chopped mixture and lemon juice in a large heatproof bowl and add 900 ml (1½ pints) boiling water. Cook, uncovered, on HIGH for 15 minutes.

*4* Strain the mixture through a sieve into another large bowl and press the cooked pulp until all the juice is squeezed out. Discard the pulp. Stir the shredded rind into the hot juice and cook on HIGH for 15 minutes or until the rind is tender, stirring occasionally. Stir in the sugar until dissolved.

*5* Cook on HIGH for about 10 minutes or until setting point is reached, stirring once during cooking. Stir in the butter. Remove any scum with a slotted spoon.

*6* Leave to cool for 15 minutes, then pour into hot sterilised jars, cover and label.

# RASPBERRY JAM

MAKES 700 G (1½ LB)

450 g (1 lb) frozen raspberries

30 ml (2 tbsp) lemon juice

450 g (1 lb) granulated sugar

*1* Put the frozen fruit in a large heatproof bowl and cook on HIGH for 4 minutes to thaw. Stir several times with a wooden spoon to ensure even thawing.

*2* Add the lemon juice and sugar, mix well and cook on HIGH for 5 minutes or until the sugar has dissolved. Stir several times during cooking. Cook on HIGH for a further 13 minutes or until setting point is reached, stirring occasionally.

*3* Pour the jam into hot sterilised jars, cover and label.

# LEMON CURD

**MAKES 900 G (2 LB)**

finely grated rind and juice of 4 large lemons

4 eggs, beaten

225 g (8 oz) caster sugar

100 g (4 oz) butter, diced

*1* Put the lemon rind in a large heatproof bowl. Mix the lemon juice with the eggs and strain into the bowl. Stir in the sugar, then add the butter.

*2* Cook on HIGH for 5–6 minutes or until the curd is thick, whisking well every minute.

*3* Remove the bowl from the cooker and continue whisking until the mixture is cool. Lemon curd thickens on cooling.

*4* Pour into hot sterilised jars, cover and label. The curd can be stored in the refrigerator for 2–3 weeks.

# MIXED FRUIT CHUTNEY

**MAKES ABOUT 1.4 KG (3 LB)**

225 g (8 oz) dried apricots

225 g (8 oz) stoned dates

350 g (12 oz) cooking apples, peeled and cored

1 medium onion, skinned

225 g (8 oz) bananas, peeled and sliced

225 g (8 oz) dark soft brown sugar

grated rind and juice of 1 lemon

5 ml (1 level tsp) ground mixed spice

5 ml (1 level tsp) ground ginger

5 ml (1 level tsp) curry powder

5 ml (1 level tsp) salt

450 ml ($\frac{3}{4}$ pint) distilled or cider vinegar

*1* Finely chop or mince the apricots, dates, apples and onion, or chop them in a food processor.

*2* Put all the ingredients in a large heatproof bowl and mix together well.

*3* Cook, uncovered, on HIGH for 25–30 minutes or until the mixture is thick and has no excess liquid. Stir frequently during cooking, taking particular care to stir more frequently during the last 10 minutes.

*4* Pour into hot sterilised jars, cover and label. Store the chutney for at least 2 months before serving.

# Sweetcorn Relish

**MAKES ABOUT 750 G (1½ LB)**

3 corn on the cob

2 medium onions, skinned and chopped

1 small green pepper, seeded and chopped

15 ml (1 tbsp) wholegrain mustard

5 ml (1 level tsp) ground turmeric

30 ml (2 level tbsp) plain flour

100 g (4 oz) light soft brown sugar

300 ml (½ pint) white wine vinegar

pinch of salt

*1* Remove the husks and silks from the corn cobs, then wrap immediately in grease-proof paper. Cook on HIGH for 8–10 minutes or until tender, turning over halfway through cooking. Strip the corn from the cobs.

*2* Put all the remaining ingredients in a large heatproof bowl and cook on HIGH for 5–7 minutes or until boiling, stirring once.

*3* Add the corn to the rest of the ingredients and continue to cook on HIGH for 6–7 minutes until slightly reduced and thickened.

*4* Pour into hot sterilised jars, cover and label. Store the chutney for at least 2 months before serving.

# Mango Chutney

**MAKES ABOUT 450 G (1 LB)**

3 mangoes, peeled, stoned and chopped

2.5 cm (1 inch) piece of fresh root ginger, peeled and chopped

1 small green chilli, seeded and chopped

100 g (4 oz) light soft brown sugar

200 ml (7 fl oz) distilled or cider vinegar

2.5 ml (½ level tsp) ground ginger

1 garlic clove, skinned and crushed

*1* Put all the ingredients in a large heatproof bowl and cook on HIGH for 5 minutes or until the sugar has dissolved, stirring occasionally.

*2* Continue to cook, uncovered, on HIGH for 15 minutes or until thick and well reduced. Stir two or three times during the first 10 minutes of cooking and after every minute for the last 5 minutes to prevent the surface of the chutney from drying out.

*3* Pour into hot sterilised jars, cover and label. Store for 3 months before eating.

## THREE-PEPPER RELISH

**MAKES ABOUT 350 G (12 OZ)**

1 medium onion, skinned and chopped

2 red peppers, seeded and chopped

1 red chilli, chopped

30 ml (2 tbsp) vegetable oil

2 garlic cloves, skinned and thinly sliced

15 ml (1 level tbsp) light soft brown sugar

30 ml (2 tbsp) lime juice

15 ml (1 tbsp) Hoisin sauce

15 ml (1 level tbsp) paprika

pinch of salt

*1* Put all the ingredients in a large heatproof bowl and mix thoroughly.

*2* Cook on HIGH for 10–15 minutes or until the vegetables are soft, stirring from time to time.

*3* Pour into a hot sterilised jar, and cover and label. The relish can be stored in the refrigerator for up to 2 weeks.

## CARROT AND RAISIN CHUTNEY

**MAKES ABOUT 450 G (1 LB)**

450 g (1 lb) carrots, peeled and coarsely grated

100 g (4 oz) raisins

15 ml (1 level tbsp) black poppy seeds

2 bay leaves

2.5 ml ($\frac{1}{2}$ level tsp) ground mixed spice

2.5 ml ($\frac{1}{2}$ level tsp) ground ginger

4 black peppercorns

50 g (2 oz) light soft brown sugar

300 ml ($\frac{1}{2}$ pint) white wine vinegar

*1* Put all the ingredients in a large heatproof bowl and cook on HIGH for 12–15 minutes or until the carrots are tender and the liquid has evaporated.

*2* Pour into a hot sterilised jar. Cover with an airtight and vinegar-proof top and label.

# GLOSSARY

ARCING This happens when a dish or utensil made of metal, or with any form of metal trim or decoration, is used in the microwave. The metal reflects the microwaves and produces a blue spark. This is known as arcing. If this happens the cooker should be switched off immediately because arcing can damage the cooker magnetron.

ARRANGING FOOD Arranging food in a circle, with the centre left empty, will provide the best results when cooking in a microwave. This is because the 'hole' left in the centre creates a greater surface area of food for the microwaves to penetrate. Unevenly shaped food, such as chops, broccoli and asparagus, should be arranged with the thinner parts or more delicate areas towards the centre.

AUTOMATIC PROGRAMMING This is a feature of some microwave cookers which allows more than one power setting to be programmed into the cooker at once, so that a number of cooking sequences can be carried out on the one setting. The cooker can be programmed, say, to start off cooking the food at a HIGH setting, then to complete the cooking on a LOW setting; to come on at a set time and cook the food so that it is ready when you come home; or to thaw food and then automatically switch to a setting for cooking. As cooking in a microwave is so fast and should be watched most of the time, this is purely an additional selling feature.

BROWNING DISHES AND GRIDDLES These are made of a special material which absorbs microwave energy. They are heated empty in the microwave cooker for 5–8 minutes, or according to the manufacturer's instructions, during which time they get very hot. The food is then placed on the hot surface and is immediatcly seared and browned. Always wear oven gloves when handling browning dishes as they get very hot.

BROWNING ELEMENT OR GRILL This device works in the same way as a conventional grill. It is especially useful for those for whom the microwave is their main or sole cooking appliance since there is no need to transfer a dish from the microwave to a conventional grill for browning. It is obviously not necessary for those who already have a grill.

CLEANING It is important to clean the interior of a microwave cooker each time it is used as any spillage will absorb microwave energy and slow down the cooking next time you use the cooker. Cleaning is easy; just wipe with a damp cloth.

COOKING TIME Always undercook dishes rather than overcook. An undercooked dish can be returned to the cooker for a few extra minutes if necessary, but overcooked food will be dry and this cannot be rectified. When following recipes, always take into account any further instructions, such as 'cook until tender' or 'until thickened'. Foods with a high moisture content will take longer to cook or reheat than drier foods, and foods which are high in fat or sugar will cook or reheat more quickly than those which are low in these ingredients. Various other factors affect cooking times, such as whether the ingredients are warm or cold, whether you have just used the cooker and the floor is still warm, the type of cookware used or the quantity of food.

COOKWARE You will find that much of your standard cookware is suitable for microwave use provided that it is not metal. Watch out, though, for items with a gold or silver trim, which will deflect microwaves, and for certain types of earthenware which may contain metal particles. Materials like ovenglass and china work well in microwave cookers but in general the best materials are those designed specifically for microwave use and which will transmit microwave energy as efficiently as possible. Although microwaves are not absorbed by the cooking dish, it may become hot during cooking because heat is conducted from the food to the container. This happens during long periods of cooking or when cooking foods containing a high proportion of sugar or fat, since microwaves are attracted to fat and sugar. For this reason, less durable containers, such as those made of soft plastics, paper or wicker, should be reserved for brief cooking times such as are required for warming or reheating bread rolls.

COOKWARE SHAPES The shape of your cookware is important because of the patterns in which the microwaves move around the cooker cavity. Round containers are preferable to square ones as they have no corners in which clusters of microwaves can concentrate, overcooking the food at these points. Straight sides to containers are more efficient than sloping ones, which cause food at the shallower outer edge to cook more quickly. A ring-shaped container will always give the best results as the microwave energy can enter from both sides as well as the top, giving more even cooking.

COOKWARE SIZES The depth of the container used is also important. Foods cooked in shallow dishes cook more quickly than those in deep dishes. Choose cooking dishes large enough to hold the quantity of food and avoid overfilling which can cause spillage and prevent even cooking. Dishes should be large enough to hold foods such as fish, chicken joints or chops in a single layer.

COVERING FOOD Cover food if a moist, even heat is required. Roasting bags, absorbent kitchen paper, a plate or a lid are all suitable for covering food in the microwave. Roasting bags should be pierced or slit to allow the build-up of steam to escape during cooking. They should be tied with non-metalic ties. It is recommended that the use of cling film should be avoided in microwave cooking, as it has been found that some of the di-ez-ethyhexledipate (DEHA) used to soften cling film can migrate into the food during cooking. Foil should also not be used during cooking as it can easily cause ARCING but it is useful for wrapping meat during STANDING TIME.

DENSITY A dense food such as meat will take longer to thaw, reheat or cook than porous, light and airy foods such as bread, cakes and puddings. This is because microwaves cannot penetrate as deeply into denser, heavier foods.

GRILLING Foods such as gratins which do not brown in the microwave may be browned under a preheated grill after cooking. Remember to cook the food in a flameproof dish and not a microwave container if you intend to do this.

MEMORY CONTROLS With a memory control it is possible to begin cooking on HIGH and then automatically switch to LOW partway through cooking time. Most cooker memories allow you to programme two or three power settings, cooking for different times or to different temperatures. Some can be programmed to keep food at a required temperature for a set length of time.

MICROWAVE THERMOMETER This is useful for cooking meat in cookers not equipped with a temperature probe, and replaces a conventional meat thermometer which (because of its mercury content) cannot be used in a microwave cooker. A conventional meat thermometer should only be used *after* food is cooked.

PRICKING AND SLASHING Foods with a skin or membrane, such as whole fish, tomatoes, liver, egg yolks and jacket potatoes, should be pricked or slashed to prevent them bursting during cooking. Egg yolks can be pricked without breaking them.

POWER OUTPUT This refers to the wattage of the cooker. Look in your manufacturer's handbook to find the power output of your cooker.

QUANTITIES The larger the amount of food being cooked, the longer it will take to cook. As a general guideline, allow about one third to one half extra cooking time when doubling the ingredients. When cooking quantities are halved, decrease the cooking time by slightly more than half the time allowed for the full quantity of that food.

REPOSITION Foods such as meatballs may be repositioned during cooking as foods on the outside of the dish will cook more quickly than those in the centre. Move food from the outside of the dish towards the centre, and those from the centre to the outside of the dish.

ROASTING RACK Specially designed for using in the microwave, a microwave roasting rack is not only useful for elevating meat and poultry above their own juices during cooking but cakes can also be placed on one to allow the microwaves to circulate underneath in order to cook the cake more evenly.

ROTATING Foods that cannot be stirred because it would spoil the arrangement, or which cannot be repositioned or turned over, such as large cakes, can be evenly cooked by rotating the dish once or twice during the cooking time. This is usually necessary even when the cooker has a turntable. It is particularly important if you find that cakes rise unevenly or if your cooker has hot or cold spots where food cooks at a faster or slower rate than elsewhere in the cooker.

SEASONING Salt, if sprinkled directly on to foods such as meat, fish and vegetables,

toughens the food and makes it dry out. It is therefore best to add salt after cooking.

STANDING TIME Many foods, especially meat joints, poultry and cakes, benefit from standing after they have been removed from the microwave cooker as this time helps to finish off the cooking process. During standing time, food is no longer being cooked by microwave energy but by the conduction of heat towards the centre. Wrap meat in foil during standing time to keep in the heat.

STIRRER Most microwave cookers have a built in 'stirrer' positioned behind a splatter guard or cover in the roof of the cooker. This has the same effect as a turntable; it circulates microwaves evenly throughout the cooker.

STIRRING AND WHISKING Since the outer edges of food normally cook first in a microwave cooker, stir from the outside of the dish towards the centre to produce an evenly cooked result.

TEMPERATURE OF FOOD The initial temperature of the food to be cooked will affect the cooking and reheating times of all foods. Food cooked straight from the refrigerator will therefore take longer than food at room temperature. For the recipes in this book, food is assumed to be at room temperature unless otherwise stated.

TEMPERATURE PROBE/FOOD SENSOR A temperature probe is used to cook joints of meat and poultry in the microwave. It enables you to control cooking by the internal temperature of the food, rather than by time. The probe is inserted into the thickest part of the food being cooked and the other end is plugged into a special socket in the cooker cavity. The desired temperature is then selected. When the internal temperature reaches the pre-set level, the cooker switches itself off. It is, however, important that the probe is inserted in the thickest part of the flesh and not near a bone as this would cause it to give a misleading temperature reading. For this reason, conventional thermometers inserted in food after cooking, or conventional techniques for testing to see if food is cooked, are usually more reliable than probes or food sensors.

THAWING When thawing in a microwave it is essential that the ice is melted slowly, so that the food does not begin to cook on the outside before it is completely thawed through to the centre. To prevent this happening, food must be allowed to 'rest' between bursts of microwave energy. This is especially important with large items. An AUTO-DEFROST setting does this automatically by pulsing the energy on and off, but it can be done manually, if your cooker does not have an automatic defrost control, by using the LOW or DEFROST SETTING.

TURNING OVER Single items thicker than 6 cm (2½ inches) will cook more evenly if they are turned over once during cooking, because the microwave signal is stronger towards the upper part of the cooker. This is particularly important when the food is not covered. When turning food over, reposition so that the outside parts are placed in the centre of the dish.

TURNTABLES To ensure even cooking, food must be turned during cooking and a turntable does this automatically. However, it is necessary to REPOSITION the food by hand. Some cookers are also equipped with automatic STIRRERS which are situated in the roof of the microwave.

# INDEX